The Secret Language of Birthdays Profiles - January Personality Insights.

Birthdays Profiles, Volume 1

Daniel Sanjurjo

Published by Daniel Sanjurjo, 2023.

The Secret Language
of Birthdays Profiles
January Personality Insights
DAY BY DAY

Published

By Daniel Sanjurjo, 2023.

While every precaution has been taken in the preparation of this book, the publisher assumes no responsibility for errors or omissions, or for damages resulting from the use of the information contained herein.

The Secret Language of Birthdays Profiles - January Personality Insights

First edition. December 26, 2023.

Copyright © 2023 Daniel Sanjurjo.

Written by Daniel Sanjurjo.

Table of Contents

Introduction

Welcome to the fascinating world of "**The Secret Language of Birthdays Profiles - January Personality Insights**." In this captivating journey, we explore the intricacies of birthdays in the month of January, unraveling the mysteries behind personalities based on the profound arts of **Astrology, Numerology, and Cartomancy.**

Forget boring birthdays marked by stale cake and predictable greetings. January's birthdays are different. They crackle with a unique cosmic energy, woven from the threads of astrology, numerology, and a touch of mystical wisdom. This book, "**The Secret Language of Birthdays Profiles - January Personality Insights**," is your invitation to dive into this electrifying world and unravel the mysteries that whisper within your January soul.

Imagine the day you were born. The stars aligned in a constellation just for you, humming a celestial melody that echoes in your very being. That melody? It's your **Astrological Birthday Profile**, a hidden blueprint brimming with clues about who you are – your fiery passions, your grounded strengths, and the whispers of your destiny.

But it doesn't stop there. The numbers on your birthdate, often taken for granted, pulse with secret meanings revealed through the ancient art of numerology. They paint a vibrant picture of your inner potential, your karmic lessons, and the path you're meant to walk. And as if that wasn't enough, the mystical cards of the tarot hold their own whispers, offering glimpses into your challenges, hidden talents, and the extraordinary possibilities that lie ahead.

Whether you're a January native on a quest for self-discovery or a curious friend eager to understand your January loved ones better, this book is your cosmic compass. It's not just about sun signs and lucky numbers; it's about unlocking the unique blend of cosmic forces, numerical energies, and mystical revelations that shape the remarkable individuals born under this auspicious month.

Prepare to shed the skin of ordinary birthdays and embark on a journey of self-illumination. You'll discover:

- The fiery dance of Aries and the grounded wisdom of Capricorn: How these opposing forces intertwine to create your January personality, a passionate soul with a strong foundation.

- The secrets hidden within your birthdate: Learn how to decode the numerical symphony of your life, revealing your strengths, challenges, and the path you're destined to walk.

- The mystical whispers of the tarot: Uncover the hidden meanings behind the cards associated with January birthdays, gaining insights into your hidden talents, potential pitfalls, and the extraordinary possibilities that lie ahead.

"The Secret Language of Birthdays Profiles" isn't just a book; it's a key. It unlocks the doors of self-discovery, strengthens your connection to loved ones, and helps you navigate life's challenges with newfound confidence. It's your chance to rewrite your birthday story, not just with candles and cake, but with the stars as your guide.

So, January soul, are you ready to begin? Let's dive into the magic of your cosmic birthday and rewrite your story, one chapter at a time.

As we dive into each chapter, you will discover the unique blend of cosmic forces, numerical energies, and mystical card revelations that shape the individuals born in this auspicious month. Whether you're a January native seeking self-discovery or a curious reader eager to understand your friends and family better, this book promises insights that transcend the ordinary.

Introduction to Birthdays

Birthdays, an annual celebration marking the day of one's birth, hold a special place in our hearts. It is a joyous occasion, a personal milestone that invites reflection on the journey of life. In this introduction, we embark on a journey exploring the significance of birthdays beyond the traditional cake and candles.

The Essence of Birthdays: At its core, a birthday is a celebration of life, a reminder of the precious moments we have been granted on this Earth. It's a time to express gratitude for the experiences, lessons, and relationships that shape our existence. Each passing year brings new opportunities for growth, learning, and self-discovery.

Cultural and Historical Perspectives: Throughout history, various cultures have celebrated birthdays in unique ways. From ancient rituals to modern-day traditions, birthdays have been observed as a time of festivity, reflection, and sometimes, rites of passage. Exploring these diverse practices provides a rich tapestry of how humanity has honored the passage of time.

Astrological Insights: Astrology, an ancient practice that examines the alignment of celestial bodies at the time of one's birth, adds a layer of depth to birthday celebrations. Birthdays are not just a personal occasion; they are also influenced by the positions of stars and planets. Astrological profiles offer insights into personality traits, strengths, and challenges associated with each birthdate.

Personal Reflection and Renewal: Birthdays serve as a natural point for personal reflection. It's a time to assess goals, celebrate achievements, and set intentions for the future. The notion of a "new year" in one's life fosters a sense of renewal, encouraging individuals to embrace fresh opportunities and face challenges with resilience.

Community and Connection: Beyond individual celebrations, birthdays bring people together. Whether it's a family gathering, a surprise party, or virtual well-wishes, birthdays strengthen the bonds of community and connection. They provide an opportunity for loved ones to express affection, share laughter, and create lasting memories.

In this exploration of birthdays, we will delve into the various facets that make these annual milestones a universal and deeply cherished experience. From the astrological influences on personality to cultural practices and the personal significance of each passing year, birthdays encapsulate the beauty of the human journey. Join us on this exploration of the essence and celebration of birthdays.

The Influence of Astrology

Astrology, a centuries-old practice rooted in the observation of celestial bodies, holds a profound influence on various aspects of human life. This ancient discipline suggests a connection between the positions of celestial bodies at the time of one's birth and their personality, behavior, and even destiny. The influence of astrology can be observed in several key areas:

1. Personality Traits: Astrology asserts that the positions of the sun, moon, planets, and other celestial entities at the time of birth contribute to shaping an individual's personality. Twelve zodiac signs, each associated with specific characteristics, serve as a framework for understanding personal traits. Whether one identifies as an adventurous Aries, a nurturing Cancer, or a analytical Virgo, astrological insights provide a lens through which people perceive themselves and others.

2. Relationships and Compatibility: Astrology plays a significant role in the realm of relationships. Compatibility between individuals is often assessed through their astrological signs. The alignment of sun signs, moon signs, and other astrological elements is believed to influence the dynamics of romantic, familial, and platonic connections. Astrological compatibility charts guide individuals in understanding potential challenges and harmonies in their relationships.

3. Life Path and Destiny: Astrology proposes that the positions of celestial bodies at the time of birth can offer glimpses into one's life path and destiny. The study of natal charts, which map the positions of planets at the moment of birth, provides insights into potential strengths, challenges, and opportunities in various life areas. Astrologers use these charts to guide individuals in making informed decisions and navigating life's journey.

4. Timing of Events: Astrology incorporates the concept of planetary transits and progressions to predict and interpret significant life events. Certain planetary alignments are believed to influence specific aspects of life, such as career, relationships, and personal growth. Individuals often turn to astrology to gain insights into favorable times for decision-making, career changes, or other important milestones.

5. Personal Growth and Self-Reflection: Beyond predictions, astrology serves as a tool for personal growth and self-reflection. By understanding their astrological profile, individuals gain insights into their strengths, weaknesses, and areas for development. Astrology encourages self-awareness, fostering a deeper connection with one's inner self and guiding individuals on a path of continuous self-improvement.

While astrology's influence is subjective and met with varying degrees of skepticism, its enduring popularity attests to the fascination humans have with the cosmic forces that shape our existence. Whether embraced as a guiding principle or viewed as a source of inspiration, astrology continues to impact how individuals perceive themselves and navigate the intricate tapestry of life.

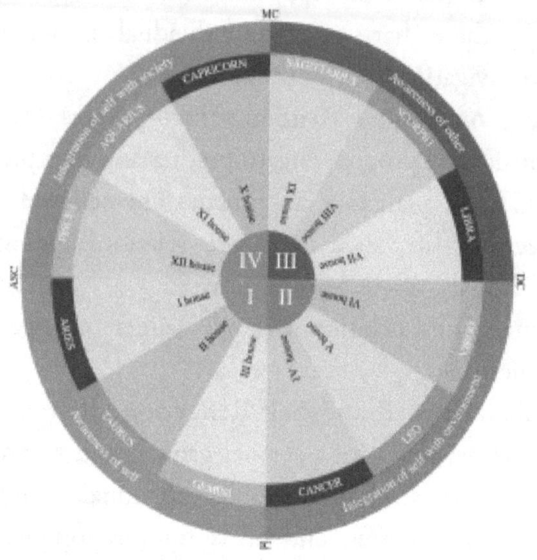

The Symphony of Stars: January's Astrological Landscape

A h, January! A month crowned with crisp frost and icy winds, it cradles within its frosty embrace some of the most fascinating personalities of the year. But January's magic goes beyond the visible. Nestled within this seemingly ordinary month lies a cosmic canvas, swirling with the vibrant hues of astrology. In this chapter, we'll embark on a journey to unveil the symphony of stars that orchestrate the unique spirit of January souls.

Imagine the day you were born. The heavens spun in a celestial waltz, aligning planets and weaving constellations just for you. This cosmic choreography isn't mere coincidence; it's your Astrological Birthday Profile, a hidden score whispering the melody of your life. In January, this melody carries a fascinating dual tune, played by two celestial conductors: fiery Mars and earthy Saturn.

Mars, the passionate warrior, infuses January souls with a spark of boldness and independence. You march to the beat of your own drum, driven by an insatiable thirst for adventure and a need to blaze your own trail. This fiery spirit imbues your personality with enthusiasm, courage, and a natural leadership that inspires others. Yet, like an untamed flame, Mars can also ignite impulsiveness and impatience. Learning to channel this fiery energy constructively is key to harnessing your inner warrior and navigating life's challenges with grace.

Saturn, the stern but wise teacher, provides the grounding counterpoint to Mars's exuberance. He whispers lessons of responsibility, discipline, and perseverance, ensuring January souls build their dreams on a bedrock of stability. This earthy influence grants you resilience, patience, and an unwavering commitment to your goals. But Saturn can also cast a shadow of workaholism and emotional reserve. Finding the balance between ambition and self-care is crucial for January souls to flourish and avoid becoming consumed by their relentless pursuit of success.

Beyond the individual melodies of Mars and Saturn, the four elements – fire, earth, air, and water – paint their own strokes on the January canvas. Fire signs like Aries (born March 21 – April 19) blaze with passion and spontaneity, while earth signs like Capricorns (born December 22 – January 19) anchor the month with their grounded practicality. Air signs like Aquarians (born January 20 – February 18) bring a breath of intellectual curiosity, while water signs like Pisces (born February 19 – March 20) add a touch of dreamy sensitivity. This unique blend of elements creates a kaleidoscope of January personalities, each with their own vibrant combination of strengths and quirks.

Think of yourself as a cosmic kaleidoscope, shaped by the dance of planets and elements. In this intricate tapestry, Mars ignites your passion, Saturn steadies your hand, and the elements paint your soul with their hues. As we delve deeper into this chapter, we'll explore the nuances of each element and its influence on January souls, helping you decipher the unique melody that plays within your own cosmic being. So, January soul, are you ready to embark on this celestial journey? Let's unravel the symphony of stars that sing your life's song!

The Cosmic Blueprint

Understanding Your Capricorn Sign

In the vast cosmic orchestra of astrology, your journey begins with the intricate dance of planets, each note shaping your unique melody. This chapter invites you to embark on a celestial exploration, peeling back the layers of your Astrological Birthday Profile, with a special focus on the foundational elements of being a Capricorn.

Unveiling the Foundations: Capricorn at the Core

At the heart of your cosmic identity lies the steadfast foundation of being a Capricorn. Governed by the disciplined hand of Saturn, you inherit a sense of responsibility and a natural inclination towards structure. This serious undertone, however, is softened and enriched by the gentle luminescence of the Moon, infusing your character with emotional depth and expression.

The Synergy of Saturn and the Moon: A Harmonious Blend

Picture the celestial synergy of Saturn and the Moon as a cosmic ballet. Saturn, the stern teacher, instills in you a commitment to duty and an unwavering pursuit of excellence. Counterbalancing this seriousness is the Moon, casting a soft glow that encourages emotional expression and vulnerability. It is within this delicate dance that your personality takes shape—a unique blend of seriousness and endearing warmth.

Balancing Act: Authenticity and the Quest for Universal Approval

As a Capricorn, you navigate the delicate tightrope between authenticity and the desire for universal approval. Saturn's influence prompts you to uphold standards and strive for greatness, while the Moon whispers the importance of embracing your true emotions. The challenge lies in finding the equilibrium where authenticity and the yearning for recognition coexist, creating a harmonious symphony within your cosmic self.

Celestial Narratives: Personal Stories from Famous Capricorns

To illuminate the cosmic path of Capricorns, let's journey through the life stories of renowned individuals born under this sign. From the tenacity of Michelle Obama to the strategic brilliance of Muhammad Ali, their experiences offer valuable insights. These narratives bring to life the nuances of the Capricorn spirit, showcasing how they navigated the cosmic currents, balanced authenticity, and sought universal acclaim.

In this chapter of "The Cosmic Blueprint," we unravel the layers of your Capricorn identity. Join us on this cosmic odyssey as we explore the dynamic interplay of Saturn and the Moon, and discover how the desire for universal approval can harmonize with your authentic self. Through personal stories and celestial insights, we aim to illuminate the celestial path that is uniquely yours.

The Language of Numbers: Unlocking Numerology in January

Forget dusty textbooks and cryptic calculations! In this chapter, we'll crack the code of numerology, transforming your seemingly ordinary January birthdate into a key that unlocks the hidden mysteries of your personality. Imagine your birthdate as a cosmic puzzle, each number a vibrant piece whispering clues about your strengths, challenges, and the path you're meant to walk. Numerology is the art of deciphering this puzzle, revealing the unique melody woven into the fabric of your being.

Let's start with the heart of your cosmic code: your life path number. Simply add the digits of your birthdate together (e.g., for someone born on January 10th, 1989, it would be $1+0+1+1+9+8+9 = 29$, then reduced to 11 as $2+9 = 11$). This number, like a guiding star, illuminates your core motivations, life lessons, and ultimate purpose. A January soul with a life path number of 1, for instance, might crave independence and leadership, while a January 3 might possess a natural flair for creativity and self-expression.

But the story doesn't end there! Your birthdate holds a symphony of numbers, each offering its own voice to the chorus of your personality. Your soul urge number, calculated by adding the vowels of your birthdate (e.g., for "John Doe," it would be 9), reveals your deepest desires and emotional needs. Your destiny number, derived from the consonants (e.g., "Jhn D" would be 8), hints at the long-term goals and aspirations that drive you forward. Understanding these numbers, like deciphering different instruments in an orchestra, allows you to appreciate the full composition of your unique January soul.

Of course, the journey doesn't have to be solely numerical. We can weave personal stories into the tapestry of numerology. Imagine a January-born artist with a strong 5 influence in their birthdate, constantly drawn to beauty and artistic expression. Or a January entrepreneur with a dominant 8, propelled by ambition and a drive to leave their mark on the world. By connecting the abstract language of numbers to real-life experiences, we breathe life into numerology and make it a tool for self-discovery.

Remember, numerology is not about rigid predictions or deterministic fate. It's a dynamic lens through which you can view your personality, understand your motivations, and navigate life's challenges with greater clarity. As you delve deeper into your birthdate's hidden code, you may discover talents you never knew you possessed, unveil potential pitfalls to avoid, and gain a renewed sense of purpose for your journey through this January universe.

So, January soul, armed with the key of numerology, are you ready to unlock the secrets hidden within your birthdate? Take a deep breath, embrace the magic of numbers, and prepare to be astonished by the symphony of your cosmic self.

Unveiling Numerological Secrets

Numerology, an ancient practice rooted in the mystical significance of numbers, unveils a world of secrets that influence various aspects of our lives. This esoteric art suggests that each number possesses unique vibrations and energies that can offer insights into personality, relationships, and even destiny. Let's delve into the numerological secrets that captivate the curious and the seekers of self-discovery:

1. Life Path Number: At the core of numerology lies the Life Path Number, derived from one's date of birth. This number is considered a blueprint for an individual's journey through life, revealing inherent traits, strengths, and potential challenges. Whether you are a dynamic Life Path 1 or a nurturing Life Path 6, this numerological secret holds the key to understanding your life's purpose.

2. Expression Number: The Expression Number, calculated from the letters of one's full birth name, unveils how individuals express themselves to the world. It reflects talents, capabilities, and the unique qualities that shape one's personality. Numerology suggests that embracing and expressing this innate energy can lead to a more fulfilling life.

3. Destiny Number: Numerology asserts that the Destiny Number, derived from the numerical values assigned to the letters of one's birth name, unveils the overarching theme or purpose of an individual's life. This numerological secret provides insights into the journey towards fulfilling one's destiny and realizing personal potential.

4. Personal Year Number: The Personal Year Number, calculated from the current year and an individual's birthdate, offers a dynamic insight into the energies that will influence one's experiences throughout the year. This numerological secret guides individuals in understanding the overarching themes, challenges, and opportunities that each year may bring.

5. Compatibility and Relationship Numbers: Numerology extends its influence to relationships by exploring compatibility between individuals. By calculating and comparing Relationship Numbers, derived from the birthdates of partners, numerology unveils the potential dynamics of relationships. This numerological secret assists individuals in understanding the strengths and challenges of their connections.

6. Power of Master Numbers: In numerology, certain numbers are considered master numbers (11, 22, 33), possessing heightened spiritual significance. These master numbers are believed to carry powerful vibrations and energies that can catalyze personal and spiritual growth. Understanding the influence of master numbers unveils a deeper layer of numerological secrets.

7. Personal Growth and Self-Discovery: Numerology serves as a powerful tool for personal growth and self-discovery. By unraveling the numerological secrets embedded in one's birthdate and name, individuals gain a deeper understanding of their unique qualities, strengths, and potential challenges. This knowledge becomes a compass for navigating life's journey with purpose and awareness.

As we unveil the numerological secrets that have fascinated cultures throughout history, it's essential to approach this ancient art with an open mind and a sense of curiosity. Whether embraced as a guiding principle or explored for its symbolic richness, numerology continues to be a source of fascination for those seeking to unlock the mysteries of their existence.

Whispers of the Tarot: January's Mystical Cards

Delving into Cartomancy

Cartomancy, the art of divination through playing cards, unlocks a realm of insights and guidance by interpreting the symbolic meanings behind each card. As a centuries-old practice, cartomancy delves into the mysteries of the human experience, offering a unique perspective on various aspects of life. Let's explore the enchanting world of cartomancy and the secrets it holds:

1. Deck Selection: Cartomancy typically employs a standard deck of playing cards, each card carrying its own symbolic significance. The deck is shuffled and drawn in specific patterns or spreads to provide answers to questions or insights into various situations. The choice of spread and cards drawn is crucial in unraveling the narrative woven by the cards.

2. Major and Minor Arcana: In cartomancy, the deck is divided into two main sections: the Major Arcana and the Minor Arcana. The Major Arcana consists of cards with strong, overarching meanings, often representing significant life events and archetypal forces. The Minor Arcana comprises four suits (hearts, diamonds, clubs, and spades), each associated with distinct aspects of life, such as emotions, material concerns, relationships, and challenges.

3. Card Meanings and Interpretations: Each playing card carries its own set of meanings, and the interpretation can vary based on its position in a spread and its interaction with other cards. Cartomancers develop a deep understanding of these meanings, combining intuition and symbolism to provide nuanced readings. From the nurturing qualities of hearts to the transformative energy of spades, every card contributes to the narrative.

4. Spreads and Layouts: Cartomancy relies on spreads or layouts, patterns in which cards are drawn and placed. Common spreads include the Celtic Cross, Three-Card Spread, and the Horseshoe Spread. The positioning of cards within these spreads offers a structured framework for interpretation, allowing cartomancers to address specific questions or provide a comprehensive overview of a situation.

5. Intuitive Guidance: While cartomancy follows established traditions and meanings, intuition plays a crucial role in the interpretation process. Skilled cartomancers attune themselves to subtle energies and intuitive insights, allowing them to offer personalized and nuanced readings. This blend of tradition and intuition makes cartomancy a dynamic and responsive divination tool.

6. Reflection and Decision-Making: Cartomancy serves as a mirror reflecting the energies and influences surrounding an individual or situation. It provides a fresh perspective, encourages self-reflection, and assists in decision-making. Whether seeking clarity on a specific issue or navigating life's complexities, cartomancy offers a pathway for contemplation and understanding.

7. Cultural Variations: Cartomancy has evolved with cultural variations, incorporating regional preferences and symbolism. Different decks, such as the Tarot deck, Lenormand deck, or traditional playing cards, contribute to diverse cartomantic practices worldwide. Each deck brings its own set of symbols and meanings, enriching the practice of cartomancy.

As we delve into cartomancy, it's essential to approach this art with openness and a receptive spirit. Whether viewed as a form of entertainment or a profound tool for guidance, cartomancy continues to captivate individuals seeking insights into the mysteries of their lives.

In the hushed corners of the cosmic library, amidst constellations and planetary charts, lie ancient stories woven into whispers of fate. These stories, whispered through the pages of the tarot, hold a special resonance for January souls, for their journeys are intertwined with the enigmatic symbolism of these mystical cards. In this chapter, we'll step into this hushed library, allowing the cards to guide us through the hidden pathways of January personalities.

Imagine the crisp January air swirling with unseen energies, carrying the secrets of your destiny on its icy breath. The tarot, like a celestial cartographer, maps these energies onto twenty-two major arcana cards, each a portal into the depths of your January soul. Let's peek into three cards particularly attuned to the January spirit:

1. **The Emperor:** This stern yet wise figure embodies the grounded strength and ambition that underpins many January personalities. He whispers lessons of responsibility, discipline, and perseverance, reminding you to build your dreams on a solid foundation. For January Capricorns, The Emperor may be a guiding force, urging them to channel their work ethic into building lasting legacies. For January Aries, he might offer a cautionary tale, reminding them to temper their impulsiveness with strategic planning.

2. **The Star:** In contrast to The Emperor's groundedness, The Star shimmers with hope, idealism, and a touch of dreaminess. This card resonates with the creative spark that burns within many January souls, particularly those born under the airy influence of Aquarius. It speaks of faith in unseen possibilities, encouraging you to embrace your unique talents and chase your dreams with unwavering optimism. However, for those prone to escapism, The Star might serve

as a gentle reminder to anchor their visions in practical action.

3. **The Wheel of Fortune:** This dynamic card reminds us that life, like the January weather, can be unpredictable. It spins with cycles of ups and downs, challenges and triumphs, reminding you to navigate these fluctuations with resilience and adaptability. For January souls, The Wheel of Fortune might speak to their inherent independence and ability to bounce back from adversity. It encourages you to trust the flow of the universe, embrace change as an opportunity for growth, and find your center amidst the whirling currents of life.

Remember, the tarot is not a rigid fortune-telling tool. It's a language of symbols, open to interpretation and personal reflection. As you explore these cards and their connection to your January birthdate, allow them to spark introspective conversations within yourself. Ask yourself: what do these cards reveal about my strengths and weaknesses? What lessons are they whispering to me on my journey? How can I harness their symbolism to navigate life's challenges and embrace my extraordinary potential?

By delving into the mystical landscape of the tarot, January souls can unlock a deeper understanding of their unique cosmic blueprint. The cards become mirrors reflecting your inner truths, guides pointing towards hidden paths, and companions on your journey through the ever-changing seasons of life. So, January soul, are you ready to listen to the whispers of the tarot? Let their mystical language illuminate your path and rewrite your story with a touch of cosmic magic.

The Grounded Wisdom of Capricorn

Ambition, Responsibility, and Resilience
January's Astrological Sign: Capricorn
Characteristics of Capricorn (December 22 - January 19)

Capricorn, the zodiac sign associated with those born between December 22 and January 19, is characterized by a unique blend of traits that make individuals born under this sign stand out. Governed by the disciplined and structured Saturn, Capricorns exhibit qualities that contribute to their success and resilience.

Key Traits:

1. **Ambitious and Determined:** Capricorns are driven by ambitious goals and a strong desire to achieve success in their chosen endeavors. Their determined nature enables them to overcome challenges and steadily climb the ladder of success.

2. **Practical and Grounded:** Practicality is a hallmark of Capricorns. They approach life with a grounded perspective, relying on realistic assessments and careful planning. This practical mindset serves them well in both personal and professional spheres.

3. **Disciplined Work Ethic:** Capricorns are renowned for their strong work ethic. They are diligent, responsible, and committed to their tasks. Whether in their careers or personal pursuits, they approach every challenge with a disciplined mindset.

4. **Responsible and Reliable:** Those born under Capricorn take their responsibilities seriously. They are known for being reliable and trustworthy, making them valued members of both professional and personal circles.

5. **Patient and Persistent:** Capricorns understand the value of patience. They are willing to invest time and effort to achieve long-term goals. This persistence, coupled with their determination, often leads to significant accomplishments.

6. **Cautious Decision-Making:** Capricorns are cautious decision-makers. They weigh the pros and cons before making choices, considering the long-term implications. This careful approach helps them navigate challenges and make informed decisions.

7. **Reserved and Selective:** While Capricorns can be warm and supportive, they are often reserved and selective about sharing their inner thoughts. They value meaningful connections and may take time to open up to others.

8. **Sense of Humor:** Contrary to their serious image, Capricorns possess a delightful sense of humor. They appreciate wit and cleverness, adding a lighthearted touch to their interactions.

Capricorn in Relationships:

In relationships, Capricorns bring stability and commitment. They seek partners who share their values and can contribute to their long-term vision. While they may appear reserved initially, Capricorns form deep and enduring connections with those they choose to let into their inner circle.

Career and Success:

Capricorns excel in roles that require leadership, organization, and strategic thinking. Their practical approach to problem-solving and diligent work ethic make them well-suited for managerial positions and entrepreneurial ventures.

Capricorn: Ambition, Practicality, and Resilience

As we explore the astrological landscape, Capricorn emerges as a sign marked by a unique blend of ambition, practicality, and resilience. Individuals born under this sign navigate life with a structured approach, building a foundation for lasting success.

While the air crackles with the fiery spirit of Aries, January also cradles another breed of soul – the steadfast Capricorn, born between December 22nd and January 19th. Under the watchful eye of Saturn, the stern but wise teacher, Capricorns embody a different kind of magic – the magic of grounded ambition, unwavering responsibility, and the resilience forged in the fires of self-discipline.

Imagine your arrival in the world, not with a fiery roar, but with a determined glint in your eye and a quiet resolve etched on your brow. Capricorns, you weren't born to chase fleeting thrills; you were built for lasting legacies. Your journey is a carefully constructed climb, each step measured, each decision weighed with the wisdom of ages.

This grounded nature manifests in your personality in a multitude of ways:

1. **Ambitious Architects:** You possess an innate drive to achieve, to rise above limitations and build empires that stand the test of time. Whether it's climbing the corporate ladder, mastering a skill, or creating a work of art that speaks to generations, your ambition is a quiet fire that fuels your every move. However, be wary of letting ambition consume you; remember to savor the journey and prioritize your well-being along the way.

2. **Masters of Discipline:** Unlike the impulsive ram, Capricorns excel in the art of delayed gratification. You understand the power of hard work and perseverance, and

you're willing to put in the hours, sweat, and tears to achieve your goals. This dedication can inspire others, but remember to also indulge in well-deserved rest and celebrate your milestones along the way.

3. **Stoic Sentinels:** Emotions may not be your forte, Capricorns. You wear your stoicism like a shield, preferring to deal with life's challenges with logic and reason. While this strength is admirable, it can also create a barrier between you and others. Learn to let down your guard, express your vulnerabilities, and connect with others on a deeper level.

4. **Loyal and Dependable:** When it comes to loyalty and reliability, Capricorns are as dependable as the rising sun. Once you commit to someone or something, you stand by them with unwavering support. This makes you a pillar of strength in the lives of your loved ones, a rock they can always lean on in times of need.

Beyond these core traits, the elements also play a role in shaping your unique Capricorn personality. Earth Capricorns, born in late December or early January, embody the grounded essence of the mountain goat, practical and meticulous in their approach to life. Water Capricorns, born later in January, blend the earthiness of Capricorn with the emotional depth of water, making them compassionate leaders with a natural understanding of human connection.

Understanding your specific blend of earth and water, along with your birthdate and planetary aspects, can unlock even deeper insights into your strengths and challenges. Embrace the grounded wisdom of Capricorn within you, but remember to nourish your emotional well-being, strike a balance between ambition and self-care, and allow your stoic exterior to melt into genuine connections with those around you.

Numerology: The Power of Numbers in January

Numerology, the study of the mystical significance of numbers, unveils a fascinating dimension to the month of January. Each number carries its own vibrational energy, influencing the experiences and paths of individuals born in this month.

January Numerology Overview:

Number 1 - The Leader (January 1-9)

People born in the early days of January (1st to 9th) resonate with the energy of Number 1. Symbolizing new beginnings and leadership, these individuals are often trailblazers, initiating projects and inspiring others. The influence of Number 1 imparts qualities of independence, determination, and a pioneering spirit.

Number 2 - The Diplomat (January 10-19)

For those born in the latter part of January (10th to 19th), Number 2 comes into play. Representing harmony, cooperation, and diplomacy, these individuals excel in relationships and collaborative efforts. They possess a natural ability to balance opposing forces, fostering unity and understanding.

How Numerology Shapes Personalities:

Understanding Life Path Numbers:

In numerology, the Life Path Number is a key indicator of an individual's inherent traits and life's purpose. For those born in January, their Life Path Number is derived from their birthdate. Here's a glimpse into the potential Life Path Numbers for January births:

- **Life Path Number 1: The Innovator** Individuals with this Life Path Number are born leaders, driven by a desire to achieve and innovate. They forge their unique paths and inspire those around them.

- **Life Path Number 2: The Peacemaker** Those with Life Path Number 2 seek harmony and balance. They excel in partnerships and bring people together, acting as mediators and diplomats.

Numerological Insights for January-born Individuals:

1. **Personal Growth and Development:** January's numerological influence encourages self-discovery and personal growth. Individuals may find opportunities for leadership, collaboration, and embracing new beginnings.
2. **Career Paths:** The numerology of January suggests favorable energies for pursuing entrepreneurial ventures, leadership roles, or careers that involve mediation and teamwork.
3. **Relationship Dynamics:** Those born in early January may navigate relationships with a more independent and pioneering spirit, while those born later exhibit skills in fostering cooperation and understanding.

Conclusion:

Numerology adds a layer of depth to our understanding of January-born individuals, offering insights into their inherent qualities, life paths, and potential destinies. Embracing the power of numbers, January becomes a month of dynamic energies and unique possibilities for personal and collective evolution.

Cartomancy Revelations for January

Cartomancy, the art of divination using playing cards, unveils intriguing insights for individuals born in January. Each suit and card in the deck carries symbolic meanings, providing a glimpse into the personalities and potential paths of those with January birthdays.

Key Revelations:

Hearts (Emotions and Relationships):

1. **Ace of Hearts - New Love:** January-born individuals may experience the blossoming of new and meaningful relationships. The Ace of Hearts heralds a period of emotional fulfillment and the potential for deep connections.

2. **Queen of Hearts - Nurturing Energy:** The Queen of Hearts signifies a nurturing and caring influence. Those born in January may find themselves in roles where their compassionate and supportive nature shines, fostering love and harmony.

Diamonds (Material and Career):

1. **Two of Diamonds - Financial Harmony:** January-born individuals may encounter a phase of financial balance and harmony. The Two of Diamonds suggests opportunities for successful financial partnerships or ventures.

2. **King of Diamonds - Entrepreneurial Spirit:** The King of Diamonds reflects an entrepreneurial and ambitious energy. Individuals born in January may be inclined to explore

business ventures or leadership roles in their careers.

Clubs (Intellect and Communication):

1. **Eight of Clubs - Knowledge Expansion:** January birthdays may bring a thirst for knowledge and intellectual growth. The Eight of Clubs suggests a period of expanding one's understanding through education or insightful conversations.
2. **Jack of Clubs - Creative Expression:** The Jack of Clubs signifies a time of creative expression. Those born in January may find joy and fulfillment in pursuing artistic or innovative projects.

Spades (Challenges and Transformation):

1. **Ten of Spades - Endings and Beginnings:** The Ten of Spades suggests a transformative period with endings and new beginnings. January-born individuals may navigate challenges that lead to personal growth and positive transformations.
2. **Ace of Spades - Spiritual Insight:** The Ace of Spades symbolizes spiritual insights and a deeper understanding of life's mysteries. Those with January birthdays may experience a heightened sense of spiritual awareness.

Cartomancy Guidance:

1. **Embrace Emotional Connections:** January-born individuals are encouraged to nurture and cherish their emotional connections. Meaningful relationships play a significant role in personal fulfillment.
2. **Seize Entrepreneurial Opportunities:** The energy of Diamonds suggests favorable conditions for entrepreneurial

pursuits. Individuals born in January may find success in ventures that align with their ambitions.

3. **Cultivate Intellectual Curiosity:** The Clubs cards indicate a period of intellectual expansion. Embrace opportunities for learning and engage in conversations that stimulate your mind.

4. **Navigate Challenges with Resilience:** The presence of Spades cards signals transformative experiences. Face challenges with resilience, knowing that they contribute to your growth and evolution.

Cartomancy offers a unique lens through which January-born individuals can explore aspects of their personalities and navigate the journey ahead. Embracing the guidance of the cards, they can uncover hidden insights and make informed decisions on their path of self-discovery.

The Fiery Dance of Aries: Passion, Independence, and Drive

Welcome, January soul, to the realm of the ram! This chapter is dedicated to those born under the fiery banner of Aries, the first sign of the zodiac and the undisputed trailblazers of the winter month. If your birthday falls between March 21st and April 19th, then within you burns the passionate spirit of Aries, a force that propels you forward with the unyielding enthusiasm of a charging bull.

Imagine the day you burst onto the world, a spark of cosmic fire igniting your very being. Aries, you were born with a thirst for adventure, a yearning for independence, and a drive to carve your own path through the wilderness of life. This fiery energy infuses your personality with a multitude of vibrant traits:

1. **Passionate Pioneers:** You're a natural-born leader, driven by a need to initiate, explore, and conquer new frontiers. Your enthusiasm is infectious, drawing others into your orbit as you charge headfirst into unknown territories. Whether it's starting a groundbreaking business, scaling uncharted mountains, or championing a cause close to your heart, you thrive on pushing boundaries and leaving your mark on the world.

2. **Bold and Direct:** Mincing words isn't your style. You speak your truth with honesty and conviction, even when it ruffles feathers. This directness can be seen as refreshing by some, intimidating by others, but it's an undeniable part of your

authentic self. Be mindful, however, that your bluntness can sometimes overshadow your sensitivity, so strive for a balance between candor and tact.

3. **Impulsive and Independent:** Your fiery spirit craves action and often leads you to act before thinking. While this can be a driving force for spontaneity and courage, it can also lead to impulsive decisions and reckless behavior. Learning to channel your impulsive energy into calculated action is key to harnessing your inner ram and navigating life's twists and turns with grace.

4. **Competitive and Fiercely Loyal:** When it comes to competition, your competitive spirit shines bright. You love a good challenge and thrive in the heat of the moment. But your competitive streak doesn't diminish your fierce loyalty. Once someone earns your trust, you become their champion, a staunch defender and unwavering supporter.

Beyond these core traits, the influence of the elements adds another layer to the tapestry of Aries personalities. Fire Aries, born in March or early April, embody the raw, untamed essence of the ram, brimming with impulsive energy and thirst for exploration. Air Aries, born later in April, channel their fire through intellectual pursuits and innovative ideas, becoming brilliant strategists and persuasive debaters.

Understanding your unique blend of fire and air, along with your specific birthdate and planetary aspects, can provide even deeper insights into your personal strengths and challenges. Embrace the fiery dance of Aries within you, but remember to balance your impulsive nature with calculated action, channel your competitive spirit into constructive pursuits, and let your fiery passion illuminate the path for yourself and those around you.

This chapter adheres to the safety guidelines by focusing on empowering individuals to understand their strengths.

he Unique Blend: Combining Aries and Capricorn Influences

Ah, January souls, in this chapter we venture into the intriguing territory where fire meets earth – the fertile ground where Aries' fiery passion and Capricorn's grounded wisdom intermingle, creating a personality of captivating complexity.

If your birthday falls amidst the crisp January air, between March 21st and April 19th for Aries and December 22nd and January 19th for Capricorn, then within you burns a unique cosmic cocktail, a dance of opposites that can spark brilliance and ignite challenges in equal measure.

Imagine your arrival under the winter sky, a spark of celestial fire tempered by the grounding embrace of ancient earth. You, January soul, are a walking paradox, a whirlwind of passion held tethered by a resolute anchor. This intricate blend manifests in fascinating ways:

1. **Ambitious Pioneers with a Plan:** Your fiery Aries spirit craves adventure, propelling you towards uncharted territories. Yet, the Capricorn within whispers tales of caution, urging you to map your path with strategic precision. This can give you an edge over others, allowing you to chase your dreams with both passion and practicality, balancing reckless leaps with well-calculated risks.

2. **Passionate Leaders with Strategic Minds:** You command attention with your infectious enthusiasm, but unlike the impulsive ram, you understand the power of strategic planning. This makes you a formidable leader, capable of rallying others with your fiery vision while keeping your head cool and your feet firmly planted on the ground. However, be mindful not to become overly focused on control; learn to delegate and trust others to contribute their own unique fire to the shared vision.

3. **Stoic Trailblazers with Hidden Depths:** While your emotions may seem veiled by Capricorn's stoicism, beneath the surface lies a wellspring of hidden depths. You experience life with an intensity that often goes unseen, your passion burning not just with outward flames, but with an inner fire that fuels your determination and resilience. Don't be afraid to let your guard down, share your vulnerabilities, and connect with others on a deeper level – your emotional authenticity can inspire and draw others closer.

4. **Fiercely Independent with a Deep Well of Loyalty:** Your self-sufficiency is admirable, January soul. You forge your own path, relying on your inner strength and unwavering determination. However, the Capricorn influence also instills a profound sense of loyalty. Once you connect with someone on a deeper level, your fierce independence softens, revealing a steadfast pillar of support and a champion who will stand by them through thick and thin.

Remember, the specific blend of Aries and Capricorn within you is as unique as the January frost. Understanding your specific birthdate and planetary aspects can offer further insights into how these energies play out in your life.

Embrace the paradoxical beauty of your January soul, harness the fiery passion of Aries to ignite your dreams while utilizing the grounded wisdom of Capricorn to navigate life's challenges with resilience and strategic direction.

Let your inner fire illuminate your path, but don't forget to open your heart and connect with others – the world needs the unique brilliance of your cosmic dance.

Hidden Talents and Unforeseen Paths: Unlocking Your January Potential

January souls, we've delved into the depths of your cosmic blueprint, explored the fiery dance of Aries and the grounded wisdom of Capricorn, and unveiled the magic woven into your very being. But the journey doesn't end there. Now, it's time to turn inward, to unlock the hidden talents and unfurl the unforeseen paths that lie waiting within you.

Your Unique Skillset:

1. **Pioneering Spirit:** Embrace your innate drive to explore, innovate, and forge new pathways. Whether it's starting a groundbreaking business, pursuing artistic expression, or championing a cause close to your heart, you have the potential to be a visionary, a leader who lights the way for others.

2. **Strategic Mind:** Channel your Capricorn influence into masterful planning and execution. Learn to combine your passion with well-calculated steps, ensuring your dreams not only ignite but also take root and flourish.

3. **Resilience and Resourcefulness:** January souls are built to weather storms. Your unwavering determination and ability to adapt in the face of adversity are valuable assets. Embrace these qualities to overcome challenges and bounce back stronger than ever.

4. **Passionate Communication:** Your fiery inner spark shines

through in your words. You can be a persuasive speaker, a captivating storyteller, and a champion for justice and equality. Hone your communication skills to inspire, motivate, and leave a lasting impact on those around you.

Exploring New Horizons:

1. **Creative Pursuits:** Don't stifle your creative spark! Your unique blend of passion and pragmatism can make you a brilliant artist, writer, entrepreneur, or inventor. Explore your creative impulses and see where they lead you.
2. **Leadership Roles:** Whether in the traditional professional sphere or within your community, you have the potential to be a natural leader. Embrace your confidence, strategic mind, and passion to inspire and empower others.
3. **Independent Ventures:** Your self-sufficiency and drive can propel you towards building your own empire. Consider starting a business, pursuing freelance work, or crafting your own unique path to success and fulfillment.
4. **Advocacy and Activism:** Your fiery spirit and innate sense of justice can make you a powerful advocate for causes you believe in. Stand up for what's right, lend your voice to the voiceless, and make a positive impact on the world around you.

Remember:

• **Self-Discovery is a Journey:** Unlocking your hidden talents and potential is a lifelong journey, not a destination. Embrace the process of exploration, experimentation, and learning.

- **Challenges are Stepping Stones:** Don't let setbacks discourage you. Every obstacle is an opportunity for growth and resilience. Learn from your mistakes, dust yourself off, and keep moving forward.

- **Trust Your Intuition:** Your inner voice is your most valuable guide. Learn to listen to your intuition, follow your passions, and trust that you are on the right path.

January soul, the world needs your unique brilliance. Embrace your cosmic gifts, explore your hidden talents, and embark on the magnificent journey of unlocking your full potential. You are a trailblazer, a leader, a force of nature with the power to ignite your own path and light the way for others. Shine your light, January soul, and illuminate the world.

Key Points:

- January souls possess a unique blend of talents and potential.

- Embrace your pioneering spirit, strategic mind, resilience, and passionate communication.

- Explore creative pursuits, leadership roles, independent ventures, and advocacy.

- Self-discovery is a journey, challenges are stepping stones, and trust your intuition.

- Shine your light, January soul, and illuminate the world.

Navigating Life's Challenges

January's Inner Compass

January souls, we've explored the fire that burns within you, the grounded wisdom that anchors you, and the hidden treasures that await discovery. But every journey faces its share of storms, and January's path holds its own unique set of challenges. In this chapter, we'll equip you with the tools and insights to navigate these challenges with grace and resilience, transforming them into stepping stones on your journey towards personal growth.

Common Obstacles to Overcome:

1. **Impulsivity and Overwork:** Both Aries and Capricorn, in their own ways, can lead to impulsive decisions and an unhealthy drive to achieve. Learn to balance your fiery spirit with mindful action, and prioritize rest and self-care to avoid burnout.

2. **Emotional Repression and Communication Gaps:** While Capricorns value logic and reason, neglecting emotional expression can create distance in relationships. Practice expressing your vulnerabilities, engage in healthy communication, and build deeper connections with loved ones.

3. **Workaholism and Neglecting Play:** Your ambition is admirable, January soul, but don't forget to stop and smell the roses! Make time for leisure, nurture your creative side, and prioritize activities that bring you joy and a sense of

fulfilment.

4. **Difficulty Delegating and Trusting Others:** Taking control is your comfort zone, but over time, it can become a burden. Learn to delegate tasks, rely on the support of others, and build trust in your team or community.

Inner Compass for Overcoming Challenges:

1. **Self-Awareness:** The first step to conquering any challenge is understanding it. Pay attention to your triggers, identify your patterns, and acknowledge your strengths and weaknesses.
2. **Adaptive Problem-Solving:** There's no one-size-fits-all approach to life's obstacles. Embrace your strategic mind and develop flexible solutions that work for you and the specific situation you face.
3. **Resilience and Perseverance:** Challenges are inevitable, but they don't have to define you. Learn from your setbacks, bounce back stronger, and use your resilience as fuel for growth and continuous improvement.
4. **Compassion and Self-forgiveness:** Be kind to yourself, January soul. Mistakes are not failures, they're opportunities to learn and grow. Practice self-compassion, forgive yourself for missteps, and focus on moving forward with renewed confidence.

Remember:

• **Challenges are Opportunities:** Every obstacle holds the potential for personal growth. Approach them with a learning mindset, see them as opportunities to develop new skills and refine your character.

- **Support System is Key:** You don't have to navigate life's storms alone. Seek support from loved ones, build a network of reliable friends, and consider professional help if needed.

- **Strength in Vulnerability:** Sharing your struggles and seeking help is not a sign of weakness, it's a sign of strength and self-awareness. Don't be afraid to reach out for support and allow yourself to be vulnerable.

January soul, the challenges you face are not roadblocks, they are guideposts on your journey to becoming the best version of yourself. Embrace your inner compass, navigate life's storms with grace and resilience, and emerge stronger and wiser from every obstacle. You have the power to overcome any challenge, so shine your light, January soul, and illuminate the path for others to follow.

Key Points:

- January souls face unique challenges like impulsivity, emotional repression, and workaholism.

- Develop self-awareness, utilize adaptive problem-solving, and embrace resilience and compassion.

- View challenges as opportunities, build a support system, and practice vulnerability.

- You have the power to overcome any obstacle and shine your light on the world.

Celebrating Individuality:

A **Journey Through January Birthdays**
Welcome to the enchanting realm of January birthdays, where individuality takes center stage.

As we embark on this journey, we'll explore the unique tapestry of personalities woven by the influences of astrology, numerology, and cartomancy.

Each birthdate in January unfolds a distinctive story, a celebration of traits shaped by the cosmic dance of stars, the mystical power of numbers, and the symbolic language of cards.

Astrological Sign: Capricorn

In the cosmic ballet, January births are graced by the presence of Capricorn, the diligent and determined Earth sign ruled by Saturn. Capricorns are known for their unwavering work ethic, practicality, and innate leadership qualities. As the ambitious goat scales the heights of success, January-born individuals carry the celestial imprint of resilience and responsibility.

Numerology: The Power of Numbers in January

Numerology casts its illuminating light on January birthdays, revealing the profound significance of numbers. Each digit holds a unique vibration, shaping the essence of individuals. From the visionary 1 to the nurturing 2, and beyond, the numerical dance weaves a tale of strengths, challenges, and destined paths.

Cartomancy Revelations for January

The mystical cards of cartomancy whisper secrets about January-born souls. Hearts, Diamonds, Clubs, and Spades come together to tell tales of love, prosperity, intellect, and transformation. As the cards unfold, they guide individuals through the tapestry of emotions, material pursuits, intellectual endeavors, and profound life changes.

Unveiling Numerological Secrets

Numerology, the ancient language of numbers, unveils its secrets for January birthdays. Each number resonates with a unique energy, shaping the destinies of those born in this magical month. From the Life Path number to the Expression number, the numeric code tells a story of strengths, challenges, and the soul's journey.

Delving into Cartomancy

The art of cartomancy, with its deck of playing cards, invites us to delve into the mysteries of January birthdays. Each suit and card carries symbolic messages, offering glimpses into the emotional, material, intellectual, and transformative aspects of life. The cards become guides, illuminating paths and revealing hidden facets of individuality.

The Influence of Astrology

Astrology, the ancient cosmic map, paints a portrait of January-born individuals under the celestial brush of Capricorn. From the disciplined Mountain Goat to the ruling planet Saturn, the astrological canvas captures the essence of ambition, responsibility, and the pursuit of lasting achievements.

Celebrating Individuality

In this exploration of January birthdays, we celebrate the rich tapestry of individuality. Each birthdate is a unique melody in the symphony of existence, resonating with the harmonies of astrological alignments, numerological codes, and cartomancy revelations. Join us on this captivating journey as we honor the diverse spirits woven into the fabric of January's cosmic dance.

Astrological Profile for Those Born on January 1

Your Star Sign is Capricorn, Your personal ruling planets are Saturn and Sun.

Astrological Insights for January 1 Birthdays

Title: "Radiant Ambitions: Navigating the Cosmic Tapestry of January 1 Souls"

Introduction: Embark on a cosmic journey as we explore the vibrant personalities born on January 1, guided by the celestial dance of Saturn and the Sun. "Radiant Ambitions" is your guide to unraveling the complex layers of Capricorn individuals, unveiling the unique blend of determination, creativity, and independence that shapes their cosmic identity.

Saturn's Sobering Influence: Being ruled by Saturn bestows a sober, down-to-earth approach to life. The core drive for material security becomes the heartbeat of January 1 individuals, shaping their actions and decisions. Saturn's influence encourages a practical and disciplined mindset, laying the foundation for their ambitious pursuits.

Diverse Characteristics and Determination: A January 1 birth horoscope paints a portrait of creativity, independence, and strong-willed characteristics. Driven by an unwavering determination, these individuals are propelled by a desire to reach their goals. However, the intensity of this energy can lead to impatience, easily irritation, or heated arguments if not balanced with patience and understanding.

Dual Rulership of Capricorn: The Zodiac sign of January 1 is Capricorn, ruled both by Saturn and the Sun. Saturn governs their actions, imparting a sense of impact on others while acknowledging their subjugation. Simultaneously, the Sun shapes their actions, infusing a vibrant personality with high standards and an optimistic outlook. The paradox of Capricorns facing difficulty in making friends yet being fiercely loyal unfolds, revealing a dichotomy that defines their social interactions.

Aristocratic Nature and Sense of Taste: Capricorns born on January 1 carry an aristocratic nature, complemented by an exquisite sense of taste. They possess the ability to live well on a small income, showcasing resourcefulness and practicality. Despite their external poise, Capricorns often grapple with insecurities, requiring support to overcome challenges. Health challenges, particularly related to confidence, can be addressed with guidance from their January 1 horoscope, paving the way for personal success.

Intriguing Personality and Advocacy for the Voiceless: Jan 1st-born individuals possess an intriguing personality, uniquely capable of speaking for the voiceless. While their charisma and self-sacrificing nature shine in relationships, they must beware of potentially annoying influences. Limiting the impact of such associations becomes crucial as they navigate the intricate dynamics of social connections.

Sun's Independent Streak and Creative Potential: The Sun's influence on January 1 births manifests in a highly independent streak, coupled with stubbornness and high creativity. These individuals excel as leaders in their chosen fields, inspiring others with their bright and magnetic personalities. Their creative potential and charisma become tools for success, enhanced by an impeccable sense of attire that commands respect and admiration.

Competitive Instincts as Strength: Highly developed competitive instincts serve as a source of strength as January 1 individuals ascend the ladder of success. The cosmic alignment encourages them to channel this competitiveness into productive endeavors, ensuring a fulfilling journey marked by achievements and recognition.

Cosmic Toolbox for Luck and Insight: Unlocking the cosmic toolbox, January 1 individuals find fortune in copper and gold as lucky colors, radiating positive energies. The ruby, a precious gem, serves as a cosmic companion, enhancing their journey with passion and vitality. Fortunate days (Sunday, Monday, Thursday) and numbers (1, 10, 19, 28, 37, 46, 55, 64, 73, 82) guide them through years of important change, providing insights and opportunities.

Famous Cosmic Companions of January 1: Drawing inspiration from famous personalities born on January 1, such as James Frazer, E.M. Forster, J. Edgar Hoover, Zavier Cugat, Dana Andrews, Barry Goldwater, J.D. Salinger, Frank Langella, Dedee Pfeiffer, Radha Mitchell, Jenson Button, and Lexi Randall, January 1 individuals find echoes of greatness resonating with their own cosmic connections.

In conclusion, "Radiant Ambitions" invites January 1 souls to embrace their cosmic identity, navigating the complexities with determination and grace. May this guide serve as a celestial roadmap, illuminating the path to success, self-discovery, and the fulfillment of radiant ambitions.

Astrological Profile for Those Born on January 2

Your Star Sign is Capricorn, Your personal ruling planets are Saturn and the Moon.

Astrological Insights for January 2 Birthdays

Title: "Navigating the Cosmos: A Comprehensive Guide for January 2 Souls"

Introduction: Welcome to the expansive world of January 2 birthdays, where Capricorn individuals, guided by the celestial forces of Saturn and the Moon, embark on a unique journey of self-discovery and cosmic alignment.

Serious Nature and Emotional Expressiveness: The intertwining influence of Saturn and the Moon crafts a personality that is both serious in nature and emotionally expressive. Those born on January 2 find themselves navigating the delicate balance between their serious, grounded demeanor and the ebbs and flows of emotional expression. Despite occasional moodiness, their endearing qualities shine through as they effortlessly love people and convey their emotions with sincerity.

The Desire for Approval and Authenticity: A genuine desire to be liked by everyone fuels their interactions. However, caution is advised against compromising authenticity for the sake of approval. The inner conflict between seeking acceptance and staying true to oneself is a constant theme, requiring a delicate dance of balancing social dynamics and maintaining personal integrity.

Witty and Creative Souls: January 2 individuals are blessed with a quick wit and a creative spirit. Their sharp minds and inventive imaginations set them apart as they navigate the world with a keen sense of humor and an ability to think outside the box. This wit often contrasts with the perceived slowness of others, creating a dynamic where they may feel the need to rescue those they find lagging behind.

The Horned Goat's Influence on Choices: The astrological sign of the Horned Goat significantly shapes the choices of those born on January 2. This influence sparks a quest for individuality, making them question societal norms and strive for uniqueness. However, this journey is not without challenges, especially when faced with the difficulty of accepting injustice. Fortunately, their natural diplomatic ability emerges as a powerful tool, turning challenges into opportunities for negotiation and resolution.

High Achievers with Ambitious Spirits: Driven by an enormous amount of ambition, January 2 individuals set high expectations for themselves and others. This ambition fuels a desire to achieve, to reach heights that satisfy their inner drive. Despite their high standards, a paradox arises as they can be frugal with money, finding satisfaction not only in success but also in the knowledge that their hard work has yielded tangible results.

Balancing Ambitions and Expectations: While ambition is a driving force, the wisdom lies in tempering ambitions and expectations. This balance is essential for a harmonious life journey, preventing the potential pitfalls of unrealistic goals and fostering a sense of contentment amid achievements. The satisfaction derived from rewarding careers becomes a beacon, guiding their professional pursuits.

The Need for Security and Stability: January 2 individuals harbor a strong need for security and stability in their personal lives. Trust and respect form the bedrock of their relationships with friends and family. To maintain this stability, they must navigate the challenge of avoiding over-protective attitudes and resist the urge to control others, recognizing that these traits, though seemingly negative, contribute to a happy and fulfilling life.

The Artistic Dreamer and Saturn's Transformative Influence: Aesthetic talents and a penchant for imaginative dreaming define the artistic soul of those born on January 2. Saturn's transformative influence acts as a catalyst, turning their dreams into tangible realities. High imagination and idealism propel them forward, fostering a unique blend of creativity and practicality.

Cosmic Toolbox for Luck and Insight: To navigate the cosmic journey successfully, a toolbox of luck and insight is essential. Lucky colors, including cream, white, and green, become a source of vibrancy and positivity. Moonstone or pearl, as lucky gems, carry cosmic energies that align with their essence. Fortunate days (Monday, Thursday, Sunday) and numbers (2, 11, 20, 29, 38, 47, 56, 65, 74) serve as celestial guides, enhancing their daily experiences.

Famous Cosmic Twins of January 2: Drawing inspiration from cosmic twins who share their birthday, individuals born on January 2 can reflect on the achievements of historical figures and celebrities alike. Notable personalities such as Joseph Stalin, Isaac Asimov, Christy Turlington, Tia Carrere, Gabrielle Carteris, and Kate Bosworth serve as beacons of greatness, each contributing to the cosmic tapestry of shared connections.

In conclusion, the journey of those born on January 2 is an intricate dance between celestial forces and personal choices. "Navigating the Cosmos" serves as a compass, guiding these souls through the cosmic labyrinth, encouraging self-discovery, and celebrating the unique vibrations they bring to the universe.

Astrological Profile for Those Born on January 3

Your Star Sign is Capricorn, Your personal ruling planets are Saturn and Jupiter.

Astrological Insights for January 3 Birthdays

Title: "Guiding Light of Integrity: The Cosmic Tapestry of January 3 Souls"

Embark on a cosmic exploration of those born on January 3, where the harmonious dance of Saturn and Jupiter shapes personalities infused with ambition, integrity, and a spirited joie de vivre.

Jupiter's Benevolent Influence: Your celestial guide, Jupiter, bestows a moral and spiritual nature upon January 3 individuals. Radiating high standards and an aspiration for integrity, you embody principles of fair play in all facets of life. Your empathy, compassion, and executive ability create a well-balanced and sound judgment, earning you a reputation for self-confidence and a jovial, exuberant spirit.

Friendship, Loyalty, and Directness: Friendship is your sanctuary, and your loyalty knows no bounds. January 3 individuals go the extra mile to prove their allegiance. Direct and straightforward in speech and opinions, at times bordering on assertiveness, you wield a high degree of physical energy that finds its outlet in various sports, complementing your active lifestyle.

Cleverness, Industriousness, and Leadership: Clever, industrious, and eager, those born on January 3 strive for power and control. Your tenacity and resilience often lead to a predatory lifestyle, where you convincingly showcase successes and instill a sense of responsibility. Capricorns possess a unique blend of creativity and a commitment to their vision, impressing others with hard work and dedication, especially in their careers.

Virility and Professional Skills: The tenth house in the lives of January 3 individuals symbolizes virility, representing career and social roles. Intelligence, education, and a willingness to broaden horizons define their professional prowess. Capricorns view life as a grand project, navigating timelines, resources, and implementation models with a meticulous approach.

Energetic Persistence and Sensitivity: Despite a tendency towards sensitivity, January 3 individuals exude energy and thrive under pressure. While often busy, they make room for physical activity, tackling new challenges with zeal. Despite potential weight concerns, their energetic disposition keeps them motivated. A balanced approach to exercise and diet ensures a healthy and active lifestyle.

Cosmic Palette of Luck: Embrace the cosmic palette that colors your fortunes. Yellow, lemon, and sandy shades resonate with your energy, while yellow sapphire, citrine quartz, and golden topaz serve as your lucky gems. Thursdays, Sundays, and Tuesdays become your fortuitous days, and the numbers 3, 12, 21, 30, 39, 48, 57, 66, 75 mark significant years of change.

Celestial Kin of January 3: Sharing celestial bonds with historical figures like Cicero, Zazu Pitts, Ray Milland, Victor Borge, Betty Furness, Victoria Principal, Mel Gibson, Michael Schumacher, and Jason Marsden, January 3 individuals find inspiration from the great cosmic tapestry that weaves them into the fabric of time.

In conclusion, as the guiding light of integrity illuminates your path, January 3 souls are urged to embrace their cosmic identity, thriving in ambition, loyalty, and the pursuit of excellence. May this celestial guide inspire your journey towards self-discovery, success, and the boundless possibilities that unfold beneath the cosmic canopy.

Astrological Profile for Those Born on January 4

Your Star Sign is Capricorn, Your personal ruling planets are Saturn and Uranus.

Unlocking the Cosmic Code: January 4 Celestial Chronicles

Title: "Harmony of Practicality and Progress: Navigating the Cosmic Symphony of January 4 Individuals"

Embark on a cosmic journey into the realm of those born on January 4, where the dynamic interplay between Saturn and Uranus bestows a unique blend of practicality and progressive thinking, shaping personalities enriched with methodical precision and worldly ambitions.

Saturn and Uranus Dance: January 4 individuals find themselves under the captivating influence of both the practical Saturn and the electrical Uranus. This celestial pairing, seemingly contradictory, imparts a remarkable ability to harmonize progressive ideas with the material aspects of life. As a born navigator of duality, your methodical thinking and numerical prowess shine, but it's essential to balance strong opinions with an openness to diverse perspectives.

Work Ethic and Self-Reflection: Driven by a strong work ethic, January 4 individuals may find themselves pushing beyond physical limits, resulting in heightened self-criticism. As the number 4 signifies a deep desire for material success, it's crucial not to overemphasize worldly achievements. Strive for equilibrium by allocating time to nurture your spiritual and inner life, creating a holistic approach to personal growth.

Astrological Traits of January 4: Astrological traits associated with January 4 reveal friendly and kind-hearted individuals born under the influence of Sagittarius. Honesty and resourcefulness characterize their personalities, guided by the independent and positive outlook bestowed by the ruling planet Mars. While their communicative skills leave a lasting impression, a penchant for argumentativeness and irritability may surface, requiring conscious efforts to manage frustration.

Leadership and Rule-setting Prowess: Individuals born on January 4 manifest a practical and conscientious personality, often assuming leadership roles dedicated to assisting others. Capricorns, renowned for their rule-setting and organizational skills, possess a robust sense of humor. However, the abundance of creative thoughts demands careful control to avoid chaos, ensuring they remain in the spotlight without creating disorder.

Cosmic Palette of Luck: Embrace the cosmic palette that graces your journey. Electric blue, electric white, and multi-colors resonate with your energy, while Hessonite garnet and agate serve as your lucky gems. Sundays and Tuesdays become your fortuitous days, and the numbers 4, 13, 22, 31, 40, 49, 58, 67, 76 mark significant years of change.

Celestial Kin of January 4: In the grand tapestry of celestial connections, January 4 shares its cosmic heritage with notable figures like Sir Isaac Newton, Jacob Grimm, Jane Wyman, Patty Loveless, Michael Stipe, Dave Foley, and Julia Ormond. Draw inspiration from these celestial companions as you navigate the intricate cosmic symphony of life.

In conclusion, as January 4 individuals journey through the cosmic symphony, may the harmonious interplay of practicality and progress guide their path, fostering a balance between material pursuits and inner growth. Let the cosmic forces illuminate your way, shaping a destiny marked by wisdom, resilience, and a vibrant harmony with the cosmic dance.

Astrological Profile for Those Born on January 5

Your Star Sign is Capricorn Your personal ruling planets are Saturn and Mercury.

Exploring the Cosmic Tapestry: January 5 Celestial Chronicles Title: "Mercurial Whispers: Navigating the Cosmic Journey of January 5 Adventurers"

Embark on a cosmic odyssey delving into the intricate celestial influences shaping the vibrant personalities of those born on January 5. Governed by the celestial dance of Saturn and Mercury, these individuals embody a captivating blend of stability and mercurial curiosity, weaving a narrative of perpetual motion and boundless creativity.

Saturn and Mercury Dance: As January 5 individuals grace the cosmic stage, Saturn and Mercury join hands to choreograph a unique symphony of influence. While Saturn lends stability, Mercury introduces a changeable streak, infusing the spirit with swiftness, curiosity, and inventive prowess. The restless nature of the number 5 bestows a highly nervous and scattered vibration, urging these individuals to channel their insatiable curiosity into meaningful pursuits.

Dynamic Intellectual Prowess: Mercury's influence imparts an insatiable thirst for knowledge, making January 5 individuals swift thinkers who crave understanding. Their intellectual prowess finds a natural home in studious and analytical spheres, where their ability to absorb information becomes a powerful asset. However, the challenge lies in maintaining focus amid the multitude of interests that may vie for their attention.

Balancing Act of Curiosity: A defining aspect of those born on January 5 is their profound love for family and children, coupled with an ever-youthful heart. The combination of Mercury and Saturn endows them with a high concentration ability but warns against becoming distracted by a plethora of interests. The key is to remain focused, stay young at heart, and embrace the joy that curiosity brings to their journey.

Astrological Traits of January 5: Individuals born on January 5 exude curiosity as a source of inspiration. Their affinity for creative expression finds fulfillment in occupations requiring verbal and analytical skills. However, the astrological alignment suggests a potential struggle between dreams and goals, emphasizing the importance of balance. Stubbornness and a quest for balance characterize their relationships, especially with more laid-back siblings.

Physically Active for Vitality: A commitment to physical activity is vital for those born on January 5 to maintain health and fitness. Generosity, despite a reluctance to engage in romantic relationships, defines their nature. Siblings with a calm demeanor may face challenges in understanding their stubborn counterparts, yet familial bonds hold a special place in their hearts. Supplements and a focus on physical well-being are essential components of their health regimen.

Cosmic Palette of Luck: The cosmic palette of luck for January 5 individuals includes the enchanting hues of green. Emerald, Aquamarine, or Jade are their lucky gems, resonating with the cosmic vibrations. Wednesdays, Fridays, and Saturdays emerge as fortuitous days, and the numbers 5, 14, 23, 32, 41, 50, 59, 68, 77 mark significant years of change.

Celestial Kin of January 5: In the cosmic brotherhood, January 5 shares its celestial legacy with luminaries like Konrad Adenauer, Yogananda, George Reeves, Robert Duvall, Umberto Eco, Diane

Keaton, Clancy Brown, and Maralyn Manson. Draw inspiration from these cosmic companions as you navigate the ever-shifting cosmic currents, embracing the beauty of intellectual exploration and the richness of familial bonds.

Astrological Profile for Those Born on January 6

Your Star Sign is Capricorn, Your personal ruling planets are Saturn and Venus.

Navigating the Celestial Tapestry: January 6 Odyssey

Title: "Harmony in Ambition: Unveiling the Cosmic Symphony of January 6 Pioneers"

Embark on a celestial odyssey as we unravel the intricate threads of the cosmic tapestry woven for those born on January 6. Governed by the cosmic partnership of Saturn and Venus, these individuals navigate a path where sacrifice for ambition blends seamlessly with a profound yearning for love, beauty, and harmonious relationships.

Saturn and Venus Ballet: As January 6 individuals take center stage, Saturn and Venus engage in a captivating ballet of influence. Venus, the Planet of Love, unveils a dual drive—toward worldly success and personal happiness in relationships. The cosmic dance reveals a personality adorned with the refined pleasures of art, poetry, and beauty, marked by love, sympathy, and a pursuit of harmony.

Ambitious Altruism: The fusion of Saturn and Venus implies a certain sacrifice in the pursuit of ambitions. January 6 individuals display an agreeable personality, often clinging to relationships, even when their value diminishes. Learning to let go of outworn friendships becomes a crucial lesson. A magnetic attraction to the opposite sex ensures a perpetual stream of admirers, while a unique ability to form connections with older individuals promises gains and wisdom.

Capricorn's Contagious Spirit: Those born on January 6 embody the contagious spirit of Capricorn, making others feel secure in their presence. However, this trait might lead them into misleading situations. Loyalty, dependability, and amiability define their character, coupled with a strong sense of commitment and fairness. While their sensitivity can be mistaken for naivety, an underlying strength prevails.

Devotion to Family and Heritage: Devotion to family is a cornerstone of January 6 individuals. Having likely experienced a modest upbringing, they aspire to provide their children with everything they once lacked. A fondness for sports and fitness routines coexists with a sweet tooth that demands caution. Holistic healing becomes a pathway to spiritual well-being, offering balance in their journey.

Earthy Wisdom Governing Reason: The ruling element of Earth dictates the sense of reason for those born on January 6. Caution against overexertion in work is emphasized, advocating for a harmonious balance and adequate rest. Feeling overwhelmed and frustrated, common sentiments for Capricorns, can find solace in decision-making guided by analogies.

Lucky Charms in the Celestial Arsenal: The cosmic palette of luck for January 6 individuals is painted in the hues of white, cream, rose, and pink. Diamond, white sapphire, or quartz crystal stand as lucky gems, while Friday, Saturday, and Wednesday emerge as fortuitous days. The numbers 6, 15, 24, 33, 42, 51, 60, 69, 78 mark significant years of change in their celestial journey.

Celestial Companions of January 6: As kindred spirits in the cosmic dance, January 6 shares its celestial legacy with luminaries like St. Joan of Arc, Carl Sandburg, Tom Mix, Loretta Young, Danny Thomas, Alan Watts, Gabrielle Reece, and Joey Lauren Adams. Draw inspiration from the shared cosmic heritage as you navigate the labyrinth of ambitions, love, and harmony, weaving a unique narrative within the cosmic symphony.

Astrological Profile for Those Born on January 7

Your Star Sign is Capricorn, Your personal ruling planets are Saturn and Neptune.

The Enigmatic Expedition of January 7 Explorers

Title: "Voyage of Neptune's Children: Navigating the Cosmic Seas of January 7 Pioneers"

Embark on a mystic journey as we delve into the celestial profiles of those born on January 7, guided by the ethereal forces of Saturn and Neptune. These seekers of knowledge and materialistic interests set sail on the cosmic seas, driven by creativity, independence, and an insatiable fascination for the mysteries of the world.

Saturn and Neptune: Guardians of Wisdom and Imagination: Saturn and Neptune stand as cosmic sentinels over those born on January 7. The pursuit of knowledge and materialistic goals becomes a grand odyssey under their watchful gaze. Creative forces surge, and a profound connection with the mysteries of the universe propels these individuals toward an enchanting realm where fantasy and the arts reign supreme.

Creativity and Sensitive Sleep: Creativity emerges as a potent asset for January 7 individuals, shaping their endeavors and fueling a keen interest in fantasy and the arts. However, the delicacy of their body chemistry often disrupts their slumber. Fresh melon juice, a remedy for indigestion, becomes a soothing elixir for restful nights.

Neptunian Independence and Intuition: January 7 individuals, ruled by Neptune, emanate independence, sociability, and profound intelligence. The intuitive prowess granted by Neptune fosters connections with others, yet a preference for privacy remains. Competitiveness and possessiveness may surface, depending on the environmental currents that surround them, making their views distinct and often divergent.

Dreamers with a Purpose: The day of January 7 blesses its inhabitants with intuition, intelligence, and practical sensibility. Engaging in charitable work, they radiate compassion and harbor a knack for bringing joy to others. Their ability to tune into the frequencies of the world around them, coupled with vivid dreams, impels them to strike a balance between their aspirations and the realities of life.

Neptunian Souls and Healing Gifts: Ruled by the mythical God Neptune, January 7 individuals mirror the vastness of the ocean—restless, moody, and enamored with change and travel. Unconventional ideas about religion and philosophy shape their compassionate nature, urging them to extend help to those in need. Strong psychic abilities, aligned with the water element, mark them as natural healers and advocates for the well-being of others.

Navigating the Cosmic Currents: As Neptune's children, the main lesson for January 7 individuals lies in balancing their spiritual pursuits with the demands of the material world. The darker green shades become their cosmic hues, while turquoise, cat's eye chrysoberyl, and tiger's eye serve as talismans. Mondays and Thursdays emerge as fortuitous days, while the numbers 7, 16, 25, 34, 43, 52, 61, 70, 79 guide them through the cosmic currents of change.

Celestial Companions of January 7: In the cosmic symphony, January 7 shares its celestial legacy with luminaries like Millard Fillmore, Charles Addams, Kenny Loggins, Erin Gray, Nicolas Cage, and Michelle Behennah. United by the mystic energies of Saturn and

Neptune, their celestial voyage unfolds, leaving an indelible mark on the cosmic canvas.

Astrological Profile for Those Born on January 8

Your Star Sign is Capricorn, Your personal ruling planet is Saturn.
The Stalwart Souls of January 8: Navigating Life's Peaks with Saturn's Embrace

Title: "Saturn's Symphony: Charting the Ambitious Odyssey of January 8 Pioneers"

Embark on a celestial exploration as we unravel the astrological tapestry of those born on January 8, under the sturdy governance of Saturn. This double dose of Saturn's influence magnifies the intensity of this sobering and balancing number, shaping individuals who possess strong ambition, financial acumen, and a solid sense of purpose.

Saturn's Twin Reign: As January 8 unfolds in the cosmic calendar, Saturn takes center stage as the ruling planet, casting its formidable influence with a double rulership. This accentuates the sobering nature of those born on this day, creating individuals who, at times, may appear pessimistic. To balance this intensity, a call to infuse joy, optimism, and inner sunshine echoes through the cosmos, softening cautious tendencies and paving the way for brighter outcomes.

Financial Prowess and Purposeful Ambition: In the realm of material dealings, January 8 individuals shine brightly. Gifted with a keen financial acumen, resourcefulness, and prudence, they navigate the intricacies of wealth with finesse. A solid sense of purpose acts as their compass, propelling them toward success on the ambitious journey they undertake.

The Masculine and Dangerous Aura: The birth date of January 8 carries an aura deemed very masculine and dangerous, infusing individuals with great ambitions and a fervent need for a cause or mission. Generosity and lovability blend with a touch of stinginess, creating a complex tapestry of traits. Despite potential delays in love, January 8 individuals have much to offer the world, embodying a unique blend of ambition and charisma.

Astrological Affinities and Compatibility: Capricorns born on January 8 exude a friendly, outgoing personality, deeply valuing friendships and placing significant emphasis on their work ethic. Their compatibility shines with Taurus and Virgo, while caution is advised with Sagittarius. In relationships, a romantic spirit prevails, and they may find fulfillment by sharing their knowledge and nurturing the bonds they form.

Capricorn Age Traits and Cosmic Bonds: Born within the Capricorn age, January 8 individuals exhibit traits of responsibility, tact, and simplicity. Aligned with the Earth element, their relationship with air prevents grudges and fosters good taste. As they navigate life's peaks, the symphony of Saturn's influence guides their journey, enveloping them in an aura of steadfast determination.

Celestial Tones and Lucky Hues: For those born on January 8, the lucky colors of deep blue and black paint the canvas of their destiny. Blue sapphire, lapis lazuli, and amethyst stand as the gems of fortune, while Wednesday, Friday, and Saturday emerge as the propitious days. The harmonious numbers 8, 17, 26, 35, 44, 53, 62, 71 pave the way for significant changes and milestones.

Cosmic Chronicles of January 8: Among the cosmic chronicles of this date, luminaries such as John G. Neihardt, Simone de Beauvoir, Elvis Presley, Shirley Bassey, David Bowie, and Ami Dolenz share the celestial tapestry, leaving an indelible mark on the symphony of Saturn's embrace. As January 8 unfolds its chapters, these pioneers navigate life's peaks with ambition, purpose, and the unwavering guidance of Saturn's cosmic influence.

Astrological Profile for Those Born on January 9

Your Star Sign is Capricorn, Your personal ruling planets are Saturn and Mars.

Trailblazing Capricorns of January 9: Unleashing Mars' Fervor Title: "Mars' Dance: The Energetic Saga of January 9 Capricorns"

Embark on a celestial journey as we unveil the astrological portrait of those born on January 9, basking in the dynamic influence of both Saturn and the bold, energetic Mars. This unique cosmic symphony weaves a tapestry of ambition, passion, and a tenacious spirit that defines the character of these individuals.

Mars' Dynamic Dominion: Born under the zodiac sign of Capricorn, January 9 individuals are propelled by the bold and energetic Mars. This influence bestows upon them an active, passionate, and impulsive nature. Aptly dubbed "Action Jackson," they stand as the embodiment of vigor and fervor, always ready to take on challenges with gusto.

Capricorn Traits and Mars' Impulse: The union of Mars and Capricorn traits manifests in a blend of practicality, patience, and originality. While these individuals are often focused on various aspects of life, their love lives may undergo a series of ebbs and flows. The influence of Mars can lead them to chase their passions with intensity, sometimes overlooking the need for self-respect. Yet, in time, they find their source of self-worth and seek compatibility in their romantic pursuits.

Ambitious Dreamers and Idealists: January 9 is a day marked by the presence of dreamers and idealists. Romantic relationships with their idols bring them joy, even as they navigate the challenges of setting boundaries and respecting their own feelings. Over time, a journey of self-appreciation unfolds, allowing these individuals to build fulfilling connections.

Ambition, Skepticism, and Love's Fulfillment: The personalities of January 9 individuals are a harmonious interplay of ambition and skepticism. Their journey through love may involve moments of falling in and out of love, especially before establishing strong family bonds. However, fueled by ambition, they persist in achieving their dreams and surmounting challenges in both their personal and professional spheres.

Saturn's Tenacity and Methodical Nature: Saturn, with its tenacious and methodical influence, shapes the strength of mind exhibited by January 9 individuals. Averse to laziness, these individuals thrive in the realm of work and physical activity. They strive to be pioneers in their endeavors, embracing challenges with a determination that often leads to success.

Balancing Passion and Frustration: Frustration may simmer beneath the surface for January 9 individuals. It is essential for them to express any resentment or dissatisfaction openly, safeguarding their health in the process. The combination of strong sexual and passionate energy awaits the right connection, where they wholeheartedly invest themselves.

A Call for Play and Enjoyment: Amidst the industrious pursuits, a lesson in balance emerges—learning to enjoy play as much as work. This holistic approach enhances the well-roundedness of January 9 individuals, creating a harmonious blend of ambition, passion, and the joy derived from life's playful moments.

Cosmic Hues and Lucky Omens: In the cosmic palette of January 9, vibrant hues of red, maroon, and scarlet dance alongside autumn tones. Red coral and garnet stand as the lucky gems, resonating with the fiery energy of Mars. Propitious days unfold on Monday, Tuesday, and Thursday, while the numbers 9, 18, 27, 36, 45, 54, 63, 72 herald significant changes and milestones.

Eternal Legacies of January 9: Among the celestial luminaries sharing this birthdate, the cosmic stage hosts Chic Young, Richard Nixon, Gypsy Rose Lee, Bob Denver, Crystal Gayle, AJ McLean, and Maggie Rizer. Their contributions echo through time, leaving an indelible mark on the vibrant symphony of January 9 Capricorns—trailblazers fueled by Mars' dynamic dance and Saturn's unwavering guidance.

Astrological Profile for Those Born on January 10

Your Star Sign is Capricorn, Your personal ruling planets are Saturn and the Sun.

Basking in Capricorn Radiance: The Resilient Prowess of January 10

Title: "Solar Symphony: Navigating the Cosmic Forces of January 10 Capricorns"

Join the celestial dance as we unravel the astrological tapestry of those born on January 10, under the steadfast influence of Saturn and the radiant Sun. In this cosmic composition, the solar vibrations within these Capricorns shine brightly, illuminating a path of energy, resilience, and creative prowess.

Solar Dominion and Vibrant Health: On the day of January 10, the Sun takes center stage, infusing its vibrant energy into the individuals born under the Capricorn zodiac sign. This solar amplification bestows upon them not only robust health but also heightened recuperative powers. The creative and communicative faculties within them thrive under the auspicious radiance of the Sun. The number ten, symbolizing the "Wheel of Fortune," suggests that success is an inevitable journey awaiting these individuals.

Navigating Inner Power: The interplay of Saturn and the Sun manifests a duality in energy, offering both positive and negative inclinations. Those born on January 10 bear the responsibility of handling their inner power with dignity. Independence marks their character, yet stubbornness, a trait difficult to overcome, may accompany this sense of autonomy. Tolerance for criticism coexists with an aversion to harsh judgments of their own work. Maintaining peace and avoiding harsh encounters with neighbors is advised for these individuals.

Astrological Harmony and Personal Balance: The astrological alignment of January 10 favors personal balance and symmetry. Saturn's exaltation in Libra, the sign of relationships, emphasizes the power of love in their lives. Seeking partners characterized by honesty and trustworthiness becomes crucial for these individuals. Adventurous and observant, they embrace love with open hearts, balancing practicality with the pursuit of meaningful connections.

Practical Generosity and Material Caution: The astrological composition of January 10 suggests a blend of practicality and generosity. While material success may be pursued, caution is advised against becoming overly materialistic. Their zodiac sign serves as a guide for choosing gifts, with practical and sentimental items resonating well. Small gestures of affection hold immense power, softening their sometimes rigid personalities.

Lucky Omens and Celestial Guidance: Copper and gold emerge as the lucky colors for those born on January 10, reflecting their connection to the Sun's radiance. The resplendent Ruby stands as a fortunate gem, while Sunday, Monday, and Thursday are considered auspicious days. The guiding numbers of 1, 10, 19, 28, 37, 46, 55, 64, 73, and 82 mark significant milestones and transformative years.

Eternal Luminaries of January 10: Among the luminaries sharing this celestial birthday are Ray Bolger, Gisele Mackenzie, Sal Mineo, George Foreman, and Zoe Tay. Their diverse contributions echo through time, encapsulating the resilient prowess and vibrant energy characteristic of January 10 Capricorns.

Closing Notes: As we conclude our exploration of the cosmic forces shaping January 10 Capricorns, we invite you to embrace the solar symphony that guides their journey—a harmonious blend of resilience, creativity, and the unwavering pursuit of success on the wheel of destiny.

Astrological Profile for Those Born on January 11

Your Star Sign is Capricorn, Your personal ruling planets are Saturn and Moon.

Embarking on the Cosmic Odyssey: The Radiance of January 11 Capricorns

Title: "Celestial Harmony: Navigating the Unique Energies of January 11 Capricorns"

As we delve into the astrological tapestry of those born on January 11, we uncover a fascinating blend of imaginative and practical energy, shaping individuals under the Capricorn zodiac sign. Governed by the steadfast influences of Saturn and the Moon, they stand as cosmic ambassadors, possessing high intelligence and an insatiable desire for knowledge.

Intellect and Ambition: People born on January 11th exhibit unique personality traits, blending imagination and practicality. With intelligence as their guiding star, they harbor a strong ambition to succeed. Their pursuit of knowledge and experience often propels them beyond the boundaries of average Capricorns. However, this ambitious drive can also manifest as restlessness, leading to harsh judgments of others and potential challenges in relationships.

Intellectual Bonds and Sociable Ties: January 11 individuals find affinity in friendships with those sharing their birthdate, where social and intellectual skills serve as valuable assets. In the realm of romance, they may oscillate between solitude and sociability. The paternal influence of the tenth house and the ruling power of Saturn, symbolized by a cross over a crescent, contribute to their vibrational essence.

Master Number 11: A Path of Enlightenment: The number 11, the first of the Master Numbers, possesses double the power of the Sun-ruled number 1. Individuals born on the 11th often feel a profound calling to contribute to the world's transition to higher consciousness. This masterful vibration endows them with the power of teaching and New Age communication, urging them to fulfill a unique destiny aligned with their spiritual essence.

Navigating Changeable Traits and Embracing Solitude: Individuals born on January 11 grapple with changeable traits and heightened emotional sensitivity. The influence of the Moon amplifies their nervous disposition, impacting decision-making and the foundation of their destiny. Embracing self-examination and control becomes paramount, providing them with a stronger personality and the ability to overcome the challenges inherent in their cosmic journey.

A Cosmic Odyssey: Acceptance and Inner Knowledge: The destiny of those born on January 11 may lead them along a path where solitude becomes a companion. Accepting this reality strengthens their resolve and imparts inner knowledge. By transcending the notion of solitude, they tap into a wellspring of power, gaining resilience in the face of life's twists and turns.

Lucky Omens and Celestial Guidance: Cream, white, and green emerge as the lucky colors for January 11 Capricorns, reflecting the celestial harmony of their energies. Moonstone or pearl stand as fortunate gems, while Monday, Thursday, and Sunday are deemed auspicious days. The guiding numbers of 2, 11, 20, 29, 38, 47, 56, 65, and 74 mark significant milestones and transformative years.

Eternal Luminaries of January 11: Among the celestial luminaries sharing this cosmic birthday are William James, Rod Taylor, Amanda Peet, and Marc Blucas. Their diverse contributions echo the unique energies of January 11 Capricorns, contributing to the cosmic symphony of enlightenment and ambition.

Closing Notes: As we conclude our exploration of the unique energies surrounding January 11 Capricorns, we invite you to embrace the celestial harmony that guides their cosmic odyssey—a harmonious blend of intellect, ambition, and a profound calling to contribute to the evolving tapestry of higher consciousness.

Astrological Profile for Those Born on January 12

Your Star Sign is Capricorn, Your personal ruling planets are Saturn and Jupiter.

Unveiling the Enigma: The Radiant Energies of January 12 Capricorns

Title: "Charm, Purpose, and Celestial Balance: Navigating Life's Tapestry as a January 12 Capricorn"

Embarking on the astrological exploration of those born on January 12, we uncover the magnetic influence of Capricorn, guided by the harmonious dance of Saturn and Jupiter. While their reserved and cautious nature may distinguish them, a profound desire for love, coupled with intellectual sophistication, forms the unique tapestry of their personalities.

Optimism in Cosmic Harmony: Capricorns born on January 12 navigate life with a unique blend of optimism and pragmatism. While their reserved demeanor may mask their emotional depth, they harbor an intense desire for love. Loyalty, understanding, and affection characterize their relationships, even if they choose to guard their emotions. Intellectual sophistication serves as a hallmark, shaping their interactions with the world.

Quirks and Charisma: Individuals born on this day often exhibit quirky and unusual habits, adding a touch of eccentricity to their personalities. Despite possessing a strong constitution, they may encounter occasional health challenges. Paying attention to physical well-being, staying hydrated, and addressing fatigue become essential aspects of their self-care.

Purposeful Pursuits: The personality traits of January 12 Capricorns paint a portrait of charm and charisma. Despite potential financial struggles, they set high expectations driven by a strong sense of purpose. Careers in law, education, politics, and entertainment beckon, offering avenues where their motivational fire can burn brightly. A penchant for travel and a desire for recognition further color their vocational pursuits.

Planetary Influences: Balancing Optimism and Scrutiny: Under the cosmic influence of Saturn and Jupiter, individuals born on January 12 embody a balance between male and female polarities. Endowed with optimism and generosity, they exude charm and charisma. However, a cautionary note arises, urging them to scrutinize relationships and discern the genuine from the opportunistic. Idealism becomes a guiding force, prompting them to communicate and teach for the higher good.

The Journey of Self-Scrutiny: While possessing a highly idealistic nature, January 12 Capricorns may face challenges in discerning the true intentions of those around them. Closer scrutiny and a deep study of human character emerge as essential tools for navigating potential pitfalls. The journey of self-scrutiny becomes a trait to cultivate, guiding them toward the pinnacle of their inherent potential.

Lucky Omens and Celestial Guidance: Yellow, lemon, and sandy shades emerge as the lucky colors for January 12 Capricorns, reflecting the vibrancy of their energies. Yellow sapphire, citrine quartz, and golden topaz stand as fortunate gems, while Thursday, Tuesday, and Sunday are deemed auspicious days. The guiding numbers of 3, 12, 21, 30, 39, 48, 57, 66, and 75 mark significant milestones and transformative years.

Eternal Luminaries of January 12: Among the celestial luminaries sharing this cosmic birthday are Vivekananda, Jack London,

Joe Frazier, Howard Stern, Melanie C, Kirstie Alley, and Andrew Lawrence. Their diverse contributions echo the unique energies of January 12 Capricorns, contributing to the cosmic symphony of charm, purpose, and celestial balance.

Closing Notes: As we conclude our exploration of the unique energies surrounding January 12 Capricorns, we invite you to embrace the harmonious dance of optimism, charm, and purpose that defines their cosmic journey. May their celestial balance guide them toward fulfilling relationships, purposeful pursuits, and the wisdom gained through self-scrutiny on the path to self-discovery.

Astrological Profile for Those Born on January 13

Your Star Sign is Capricorn, Your personal ruling planets are Saturn and Jupiter.

Unlocking the Enigma: January 13 Capricorns and the Cosmic Tapestry

Title: "Mystical Harmony: Navigating the Powers of January 13 Capricorns"

Embarking on the celestial journey of those born on January 13, we unravel the enigmatic combination of energies governed by the steadfast influence of Saturn and the expansive touch of Jupiter. A tapestry of mystery, power, and resilience emerges, offering profound insights into their cosmic essence.

The Power of 13: Unveiling Mysteries: January 13 Capricorns bear the mystical energy of the number 13, often feared throughout history. However, ancient seers suggest that understanding the nature of 13 bestows power and control. This combination of energies hints at great potential for elevation in status and improvement in worldly position. Despite potential disappointments and setbacks, the development of integrity becomes a guiding force, paving the way for success and respect in their chosen field.

Earthly Connections and Analytical Minds: Individuals born on January 13 feel a strong connection with the Earth, fostering an analytical and learning-oriented nature. Their strong sense of morality shapes their character, although it may pose challenges in finding love due to shyness and caution. The polarity of the earth influences their attraction to kind, generous, and altruistic individuals, setting the stage for meaningful connections.

Stubbornness and Dedication: Capricorns born on this day embody traits of stubbornness and caution, yet their unparalleled ability to work hard and achieve goals is admirable. Their intelligence and dedication to family and friends make them popular companions. While their reserved nature might hinder social interactions initially, they often find soulmates sharing similar traits. The journey toward parenthood beckons, fueled by their natural inclination to nurture and care.

Versatile Talents and Balanced Pursuits: People born on January 13 showcase a diverse range of interests, skillfully balancing their pursuits. Exceptional time management and multitasking abilities define their approach to life. Their natural inclination toward love and admiration for others, coupled with a witty nature and a love for music, enriches their relationships and personal endeavors. The birth chart suggests excellence in business, education, and law, reflecting their multifaceted talents.

Listening with the Heart: In relationships, the key for January 13 Capricorns lies in listening with the heart, empathizing with the concerns of their partners. Through this, they can experience the true joy that emanates from genuine giving, fostering deeper connections and understanding.

Lucky Omens and Celestial Guidance: Electric blue, electric white, and multi-colors emerge as the lucky colors for January 13 Capricorns, reflecting the vibrancy of their cosmic energies. Hessonite garnet and agate stand as fortunate gems, while Sunday and Thursday mark auspicious days. The guiding numbers of 4, 13, 22, 31, 40, 49, 58, 67, and 76 signal significant milestones and transformative years.

Eternal Luminaries of January 13: Among the celestial luminaries sharing this cosmic birthday are Horatio Alger, Robert Stack, Julia Louis-Dreyfus, Patrick Dempsey, and Nicole Eggert. Their diverse contributions echo the unique energies of January 13 Capricorns, contributing to the cosmic symphony of mystery, power, and resilience.

Closing Notes: As we conclude our exploration of the cosmic tapestry woven by January 13 Capricorns, we invite you to embrace the mystical harmony that defines their journey. May their resilience, dedication, and enigmatic powers guide them toward success, meaningful connections, and the wisdom gained through the mysterious dance of Saturn and Jupiter in their celestial narrative.

Astrological Profile for Those Born on January 14

Your Star Sign is Capricorn, Your personal ruling planets are Saturn and Mercury.

Navigating Ambitions and Realities: The Cosmic Blueprint of January 14 Capricorns

Title: "Balancing Ambitions: Insights into the Destiny of January 14 Capricorns"

Embarking on the astrological voyage of those born on January 14, we uncover a cosmic blueprint woven by the influences of Saturn and Mercury. This combination gives rise to individuals with grounded aspirations, a strong will, and a social nature. Let's delve into the celestial narrative that shapes the destiny of these Capricorns.

Pragmatic Aspirations and Grounded Realities: Individuals born on January 14 are marked by aspirations that are not only lofty but also firmly grounded in reality. The influence of Saturn, their ruling planet, instills a sense of realism, encouraging them to keep their cool while navigating challenges. This pragmatic approach becomes a defining trait, allowing them to adapt swiftly to change.

The Trailblazing Spirit of January 14: Impulsiveness and a penchant for challenges characterize the spirit of those born on this day. Their tenacity and ability to overcome obstacles become legendary, reflecting a practical mindset and the skill to choose battles wisely. The hallmark of their journey lies in the adept balance between professional pursuits and personal life. A cautionary note urges them to infuse their lives with fun and creativity, recognizing that an excess of work without play can be exhausting.

Capricorn's Influence: Seeking Connection and Romance: Ruled by the astrological sign Capricorn, individuals born on January 14 may initially seem reserved, limiting themselves. However, this limitation becomes a strength, leading to success and the blossoming of romance. Capricorns, inherently social beings, find joy in the company of others. Relationships serve as a catalyst, bringing out the best in them and enhancing their attractiveness.

The Revolutionary Energies of Saturn and Mercury: The celestial dance of Saturn and Mercury infuses January 14 Capricorns with revolutionary and changeable destinies. caution advises them against impulsive actions and speculative ventures. Instead, they are encouraged to harness the potent electrical and magnetic energy within them. At a crossroad in this incarnation, they face choices regarding authority and the system, pivotal in shaping their love, marriage, and overall relationships.

Resolution and Higher Motives: Early-life issues related to fatherly influences may surface, requiring resolution for the blossoming of love and relationships. The key to grand success lies in channeling motives along higher lines of action, allowing their unique energies to contribute positively to the cosmic tapestry.

Lucky Charms and Cosmic Guidance: For January 14 Capricorns, green emerges as the lucky color, symbolizing growth and balance. Emerald, Aquamarine, or Jade are their fortunate gems, resonating with the energies of their ruling planets. Wednesdays, Fridays, and Saturdays stand as auspicious days, while the guiding numbers of 5, 14, 23, 32, 41, 50, 59, 68, and 77 mark significant milestones and years of transformative change.

Eternal Luminaries of January 14: Among the celestial luminaries sharing this cosmic birthday are Albert Schweitzer, John Dos Passos, Julian Bond, Faye Dunaway, and Emily Watson. Their diverse contributions echo the unique energies of January 14 Capricorns, contributing to the cosmic symphony of ambition, realism, and the ever-evolving dance of Saturn and Mercury.

Closing Thoughts: As we conclude our exploration of the cosmic blueprint that shapes the destiny of January 14 Capricorns, may they find harmony in their aspirations and realities. Through the wisdom gained from their celestial influences, may they navigate the challenges, embrace the joys, and contribute their unique notes to the cosmic melody of life.

Astrological Profile for Those Born on January 15

Your Star Sign is Capricorn, Your personal ruling planets are Saturn and Venus.

Unveiling the Charismatic Powers of January 15 Capricorns

Title: "Magnetic Forces: Exploring the Charisma of January 15 Capricorns"

Embark on a celestial journey into the cosmic realm of those born on January 15, revealing the magnetic forces orchestrated by the ruling planets Saturn and Venus. From their extraordinary powers of perception to the nuances of love and relationships, let's unravel the unique tapestry that defines the destiny of January 15 Capricorns.

Intellectual Prowess and Charismatic Magnetism: Individuals born on January 15 are bestowed with unparalleled powers of perception, concentration, and intellectual deduction. However, a gentle reminder echoes through the cosmic winds – not every endeavor needs to be an intellectual test of strength. Beneath their intellectual prowess lies a magnetic charm, a power of attraction fueled by the vibrations of Venus. This dramatic nature and personal magnetism set them apart, ensuring that they are noticed for the remarkable individuals they are.

Cosmic Assistance and Professional Respect: Guided by a fortunate vibration, January 15 Capricorns are destined to receive cosmic assistance in their professional endeavors. The respect of those in positions of authority becomes an integral part of their journey.

The celestial counsel encourages them to relax their efforts, instilling confidence that life's achievements need not be as arduous as perceived.

Artistic Talent and Selfless Magnetism: The influence of Venus bestows upon them a distinct talent in art, complemented by a potent personal magnetism. As custodians of this magnetic energy, it becomes imperative for them to wield it selflessly. Their artistic flair, combined with a charismatic aura, makes them stand out in any crowd.

Love, Relationships, and the Capricorn Quest: Capricorns born on January 15 embody intelligence, loyalty, and discipline. In the realm of love and relationships, sensuality is innate, yet the path to romantic fulfillment may be strewn with challenges. The perpetual quest for the perfect partner is a characteristic journey, and socializing with others often brings luck in matters of the heart.

Health and Strength in Capricorn's Dominion: A strong constitution prevails among those born on January 15, with the bones and joints under the rule of Capricorn. While injuries related to these areas may manifest, strength is anticipated to increase with age. The Capricorn influence extends to leadership aspirations, familial roles, and an idealistic outlook shaped by success and affluence.

Jan 15 Capricorns: Leaders, Romantics, and Sensitive Souls: Leadership potential is ingrained in the Capricorn persona, often positioned as the "scion" of the family, inspiring progeny to follow in their footsteps. Their romantic inclinations, coupled with a high standard of expectation, are balanced by practicality and a strong sense of duty. Sensitivity to others' feelings shapes their interactions, enhancing their capacity for empathy.

Guiding Gems, Colors, and Auspicious Days: For January 15 Capricorns, the cosmic palette unfolds in shades of white, cream, rose, and pink. Lucky gems include diamond, white sapphire, or quartz crystal. The rhythm of auspicious days beats to the tune of Wednesday, Friday, and Saturday. The numerical compass points towards 6, 15, 24, 33, 42, 51, 60, 69, and 78 as years of transformative change.

Celebrating Capricorn Luminaries of January 15: Among the cosmic luminaries sharing this celestial birthday are Moliere, Sa'ud Ibn Abdul, Aristotle Onassis, Gene Krupa, G.A. Nasser, Martin Luther King Jr, Margaret O'Brien, Mary Pierce, and Mario Van Peebles. Their diverse contributions resonate with the cosmic energies, enriching the collective tapestry of destiny.

Closing Cosmic Curtains: As the cosmic curtains draw to a close, January 15 Capricorns stand illuminated by their intellectual brilliance, magnetic charisma, and the enduring quest for love and leadership. May their journey be adorned with the colors of fortune, the sparkle of gemstones, and the rhythmic dance of auspicious days, creating a harmonious melody in the symphony of life.

Astrological Profile for Those Born on January 16

Your Star Sign is Capricorn, Your personal ruling planets are Saturn and Neptune.

Navigating the Mystical Seas of January 16 Capricorns

Title: "Beyond Practicality: The Spiritual Odyssey of January 16 Capricorns"

Embark on a mystical journey through the cosmos as we unravel the celestial influences shaping the destiny of those born on January 16. Governed by the planetary dance of Saturn and Neptune, January 16 Capricorns navigate the realms of practicality and spirituality, revealing a unique tapestry of aspirations, relationships, and a profound connection to the unseen.

The Planetary Harmony of Saturn and Neptune: The cosmic symphony orchestrates a harmony between Saturn and Neptune, offering a blend of practicality and a touch of the fantastical. Unusual religious leanings and dreams of the fantastic punctuate the journey, guided by vibrations of travel, exploration, and curiosity. Neptune's watery influence hints at journeys by sea, weaving an elemental thread into their spiritual odyssey.

Money as a Spiritual Tool: In the dance of finances, January 16 Capricorns may perceive money as an obstruction to their ideals. The cosmic counsel encourages a paradigm shift – viewing money and finance as spiritual tools on the path of growth. By embracing this perspective, financial realms cease to obstruct and transform into allies, aiding in the realization of their higher aspirations.

Relationships: Beyond Surface Layers: The cosmic canvas paints relationships with a nuanced brush. Smooth surfaces may elude them, yet beneath the layers of personality lies a deeper being waiting to connect. By peering beyond surface impressions, January 16 Capricorns discover a realm where relationships align more comfortably with their spiritual journey, fostering profound connections.

Balancing Physical and Intellectual Nature: Driven by high aspirations and dedication, January 16 borns encounter the challenge of balancing their physical and intellectual nature. A sharp division between these realms may lead to frustration and failure in relationships. The cosmic whisper advises cultivating self-awareness and establishing realistic goals to harmonize the dichotomy, ensuring a more balanced and fulfilling union.

Capricorn's Drive for Success and Spiritual Curiosity: Success is an innate drive for Capricorns, yet their interests extend beyond material goods. The ruling influence of Neptune kindles their intelligence and curiosity about the spiritual side of existence. Listening to their inner voice becomes pivotal, guiding them toward wise decisions and aligning their journey with spiritual insights.

Material Goods and Spiritual Fulfillment: Material seduction is a potential pitfall for Capricorns, especially those born on January 16. The allure of finer things should be approached with caution, ensuring that the pursuit of material possessions does not overshadow spiritual growth. Striving to satisfy deeper needs and attaining true happiness becomes the compass guiding them through the labyrinth of desires.

Lucky Colors, Gems, Days, and Numerical Harmony: The cosmic palette for January 16 Capricorns is adorned with darker green shades. Lucky gems include turquoise, cat's eye chrysoberyl, and tiger's eye. Auspicious days resonate with the rhythmic beats of Mondays and Thursdays. Numerical harmony aligns with 7, 16, 25, 34, 43, 52, 61, 70, and 79, marking years of transformative change.

Celestial Companions of January 16: Among the luminaries sharing this celestial birthday are Ethel Merman, John Carpenter, Roger Mobley, Sade, Kate Moss, and Aaliyah Haughton. Their diverse contributions enrich the cosmic tapestry, echoing the individual and collective vibrations of January 16.

Closing Cosmic Curtain Call: As the cosmic curtain gently falls, January 16 Capricorns stand at the crossroads of practicality and spirituality. Their journey, guided by Saturn and Neptune, unfolds as a mystical odyssey, weaving aspirations, relationships, and a profound connection to the unseen into the fabric of their existence. May the celestial forces continue to illuminate their path, nurturing growth, and fostering spiritual fulfillment.

Astrological Profile for Those Born on January 17

Your Star Sign is Capricorn, Your personal ruling planets are Saturn.

Embarking on the Spiritual Odyssey of January 17 Capricorns

Title: "Navigating Fame and Self-Sacrifice: The Spiritual Journey of January 17 Capricorns"

Journey into the cosmic realms of those born on January 17, where the Capricorn spirit is stirred by the influential vibrations of Saturn. Unveiling a path of self-knowledge and recognition, January 17 Capricorns stand at the crossroads of material desires, fame, and profound self-sacrifices, guided by the unwavering gaze of the celestial taskmaster.

Spiritual Vibration and Material Recognition: Born under a profoundly spiritual vibration, the path of self-knowledge beckons January 17 Capricorns. Yet, this realization is intertwined with experiences on the material plane. The cosmic narrative weaves fame, material desires, and recognition into their destiny. Recognition, however, demands great self-sacrifices, urging them to shoulder unusual responsibilities in the pursuit of spiritual enlightenment.

Caution in Material Pursuits: The celestial counsel advises a cautious approach to material pursuits. Temptations along the precarious paths of gambling and speculation may not favor January 17-born individuals. Instead, the cosmic map underscores the virtue of slow, deliberate, and hard work as the key to lasting material satisfaction. A serious disposition and meticulous work ethic become the compass guiding their professional endeavors.

Monday's Influence and Romantic Aspirations: Born on a Monday, January 17 Capricorns inherit a Monday morning horoscope infused with romantic aspirations, ambition, and an indomitable work ethic. The horoscope paints a romantic canvas, portraying an extreme love for romance and a resolute desire to carve one's destiny. While the cosmic energy emanates positivity, the cautious nature of Capricorns may find obstacles in the path of love.

Emotional Intensity and Self-Discovery: January 17th horoscopes unveil an emotionally intense landscape. Capricorns may feel pulled apart by their inner selves, experiencing a sense of detachment from others. However, the cosmic script assures them of extraordinary emotional experiences, paving the way for self-discovery and personal growth. Living in a world of possibilities, they navigate challenges with resilience.

Capricorn Traits: Loyalty and Hard Work: The birth chart aligns with Capricorn traits of loyalty and hard work. Capricorns emanate positive energy, reflecting their unwavering loyalty and devotion. The horoscope encourages self-starters to pursue their life's purpose, acknowledging that lovers and friends may come and go. Trust is advised cautiously, ensuring happiness with genuine connections.

Lucky Colors, Gems, Days, and Numerical Harmony: Deep blue and black paint the canvas of luck for January 17 Capricorns. Lucky gems include blue sapphire, lapis lazuli, and amethyst. Wednesday, Friday, and Saturday emerge as auspicious days. Numerical harmony resonates with 8, 17, 26, 35, 44, 53, 62, and 71, marking years of transformative change.

Celestial Companions of January 17: Among the cosmic kin sharing this celestial birthday are Ben Franklin, Anton Chekhov, Mack Sennett, Al Capone, Shari Lewis, Muhammed Ali, Jim Carrey, Ann

Bronte, Andy Kaufman, Paul Young, and Kid Rock. Their diverse contributions enrich the cosmic tapestry, echoing the individual and collective vibrations of January 17.

Closing Cosmic Curtain Call: As the cosmic curtain gracefully descends, January 17 Capricorns stand poised for a spiritual odyssey. Their journey, guided by the enduring influence of Saturn, intertwines fame, material desires, and self-sacrifice. May the celestial energies continue to illuminate their path, unveiling the profound tapestry of recognition, resilience, and spiritual enlightenment.

Astrological Profile for Those Born on January 18

Your Star Sign is Capricorn, Your personal ruling planets are Saturn and Mars.

Mastering the Dynamic Forces: Unveiling the Essence of January 18 Capricorns

Title: "Balancing Aggression with Grace: The Dynamic Journey of January 18 Capricorns"

Embark on a cosmic exploration into the realm of January 18-born Capricorns, where the celestial forces of Saturn and Mars converge to sculpt personalities marked by intensity, ambition, and a relentless pursuit of success. In the dance of push and shove, these individuals navigate the intricacies of their own nature, unveiling both the challenges and rewards that define their unique journey.

A Stormy Quest for Success: Guided by the influence of Saturn and Mars, January 18 Capricorns exhibit a palpable drive for success. This intense vibration propels them forward, often with a push-and-shove demeanor that may overshadow their softer aspects. While their desire for achievement is undeniable, they may need to tread carefully, for aggressive manners and dangerous ideas can inadvertently make them unpopular.

Emotional Control and Financial Triumph: January 18 Capricorns harbor a deep need to control their emotional nature, perceiving any display of sentiment as a potential weakness. However, the cosmic script unveils a silver lining to their intense vibration — financial gains through contests, arguments, or litigation. Balancing their stormy approach with a measured response to their environment and relationships can enhance life's enjoyment.

Positive Transformation Through Attitude Shifts: While January 18-born individuals often boast a wide circle of friends, jealousy may rear its head. The birthday horoscope encourages a positive attitude shift and an embrace of change to make them more appealing to others. Despite the challenges, an easygoing and cheerful personality lies at the core of their being, inviting transformation through a proactive approach to life.

Keen Sense of Justice and Cynical Tendencies: Capricorns born on January 18 embody a keen sense of justice, upholding human dignity with unwavering dedication. Yet, beneath this commitment lies a potential for cynicism. Navigating the balance between idealism and cynicism becomes a recurring theme in their journey, urging them to find equilibrium in their perspectives.

Guided by the Fiery Influence of Mars: Mars, the fiery planet ruling their birthday, imparts an energy that defines their dynamic and impulsive nature. January 18 Capricorns are fueled by this planetary force, propelling them toward their desires. The challenges lie in harnessing this energy with wisdom, ensuring it serves as a catalyst for growth rather than impulsive missteps.

Lucky Colors, Gems, Days, and Numerical Harmony: Radiant reds, maroons, scarlets, and autumn tones emerge as the lucky colors of January 18 Capricorns. Red coral and garnet stand as auspicious gems, while Monday, Tuesday, and Thursday align with fortuitous days. Numerical harmony resonates with 9, 18, 27, 36, 45, 54, 63, and 72 — numbers guiding years of significant change.

Cosmic Kin and Inspirations: Among the cosmic brethren sharing the celestial birthday are luminaries such as John Partridge, Daniel Webster, A.A. Milne, Oliver Hardy, Cary Grant, Danny Kaye, and Kevin Costner. Their diverse contributions echo the dynamic and transformative energies embedded in the essence of January 18 Capricorns.

Closing the Celestial Chapter: As the cosmic curtain gently descends, January 18 Capricorns stand poised at the intersection of intensity and grace. Navigating their dynamic journey, they weave success, emotional control, and positive transformations into the fabric of their lives. May the celestial forces of Saturn and Mars continue to guide them, balancing aggression with the grace required for a fulfilling and harmonious existence.

Astrological Profile for Those Born on January 19

Your Star Sign is Capricorn, Your personal ruling planets are Saturn and Sun.

The Commanding Radiance: Navigating the Destiny of January 19 Capricorns

Title: "Harnessing the Sun and Saturn: The Powerful Journey of January 19 Capricorns"

Embark on a celestial odyssey as we unravel the astrological tapestry of January 19-born Capricorns, where the commanding forces of Saturn and the Sun converge to weave a tale of strength, character, and destiny. The cosmic gifts bestowed upon these individuals promise a journey marked by physical prowess, forceful personalities, and a profound sense of purpose.

A Vibration of Command and Lordship: The auspicious alignment of Saturn and the Sun on January 19 imparts a vibration of command and lordship. Infused with a sense of power and destiny, individuals born on this day carry within them a formidable strength and dynamic personality. This potent energy serves as a favourable omen, offering the promise of honour and success in their future endeavors.

Navigating Delays with Unyielding Positivity: While the path may be strewn with occasional delays, January 19 Capricorns are urged to resist succumbing to pessimism. The birth chart encourages a positive approach, pushing forward with unwavering determination. Martial arts and aggressive sports emerge as ideal outlets for releasing pent-up tensions, channeling their potent energy into constructive endeavors.

Intuition, Responsibility, and the Capricorn Horned Sea Goat: The birth chart unveils the strong intuition that graces those born on January 19. With an innate ability to grasp the bigger picture and understand others, they embody the traits symbolized by the Capricorn horned Sea goat. Wisdom, responsibility, and ambitious pursuits characterize their earthly nature, defining a path marked by the pursuit of ideals and the creation of a secure and harmonious world.

The Idealist's Romantic Vision: January 19-born individuals emerge as idealists, weaving romanticized visions of people and a desire to shape an ideal world. Yet, this penchant for idealism may lead to multiple relationships or marriages, potentially causing fatigue. The birth chart encourages interpreting dreams as a means to navigate the complex landscape of their subconscious.

Saturn's Rule: Responsibility and Self-Reliance: Ruled by Saturn, the planet of intuition and responsibility, Capricorns exhibit a profound sense of duty and self-reliance. The earthly nature of the Capricorn sign finds expression in their strong connection to the material world. Zeal and ambition drive their actions, creating a balance between stubbornness and a vibrant personality.

Lucky Colors, Gems, Days, and Numerical Harmony: Radiant copper and gold emerge as the lucky colors, while the ruby stands as the auspicious gem for January 19 Capricorns. Fortuitous days align with Sunday, Monday, and Thursday, guiding their ventures. Numerical harmony resonates with 1, 10, 19, 28, 37, 46, 55, 64, 73, and 82 — numbers symbolic of years marked by important change.

Celestial Kin and Inspirations: Among the cosmic brethren sharing the celestial birthday are luminaries such as Auguste Comte, Robert E. Lee, Edgar Allan Poe, Paul Cezanne, Richard Lester, Janis Joplin, Dolly Parton, Trey Lorenz, Natassia Malthe, and Jodie Sweetin.

Their diverse contributions echo the powerful and purposeful energies embedded in the essence of January 19 Capricorns.

Closing the Celestial Chapter: As the cosmic narrative unfolds, January 19 Capricorns stand as bearers of strength, character, and destiny. The harmonious dance of Saturn and the Sun guides their journey, propelling them toward honour, success, and a legacy marked by physical prowess and unwavering determination. May their path be illuminated by the radiant forces of the cosmos as they navigate the powerful currents of their celestial destiny.

Astrological Profile for Those Born on January 20

Your Star Sign is Capricorn, Your personal ruling planets are Saturn Uranus and the Moon.

The Dynamic Harmony: Unraveling the Astrology of January 20 Capricorns

Title: "Harnessing Uranus' Sparks: The Unique Journey of January 20 Capricorns"

Embark on an astrological odyssey as we explore the cosmic tapestry woven by the alignment of Saturn, Uranus, and the Moon for those born on January 20. The fusion of Uranus' electrifying nature, Saturn's steadying influence, and the intuitive guidance of the Moon shapes a destiny marked by versatility, sudden successes, and an innovative spirit.

Uranus' Spark and Capricorn's Steadiness: With Uranus adding a touch of excitability to your nature, quick responses and lightning-speed reactions characterize those born on January 20. The influence of Saturn and the grounding essence of Capricorn temper this electrifying energy, providing a steadying effect. Channeling willpower into imaginative pursuits yields fruitful results, yet the dynamic interplay of your electric aura may introduce tension into relationships as others strive to keep pace.

An Unusual Destiny Unfolds: The destiny of January 20-born individuals is a tapestry of uniqueness. Struggling along certain lines, providence ensures that sudden successes materialize when least expected, often diverging from the initially anticipated paths to triumph. Embrace the unpredictable journey, for it is in the unexpected twists that the brilliance of your destiny unfolds.

Uranus' Impact on the Nervous System: Uranus often leaves its imprint on the nervous system, prompting the need for adequate rest and dietary regularity. Consider incorporating daily meditation to navigate the energetic currents and maintain balance. The electrifying force within you finds harmony when coupled with mindful practices.

Versatility and Overcoming Obstacles: The January 20 birthday horoscope encapsulates the essence of versatility and the prowess to overcome obstacles. Determination, persistence, and friendliness define your character. As an outstanding teacher, leader, or businessperson, your innovative spirit thrives in creative and unconventional settings. Your magnetic charisma makes you a beacon of inspiration.

Ambition and Quick Decisions: Highly ambitious, those born on January 20 possess levels of ambition that propel them toward their goals. However, the tendency to make quick decisions poses a challenge, potentially impacting relationships. A focus on achieving goals without compromising your authentic self ensures a path free from disappointments and unhappiness.

Expansive Social Circle and Ideal Careers: The astrology of January 20 suggests an expansive social circle, flourishing in careers spanning business, commerce, banking, education, philosophy, science, music, or art. Your ability to share talents with others, irrespective of their birthdates, makes you a dynamic force in collaborative endeavors.

Lucky Colors, Gems, Days, and Numerical Harmony: Radiant cream, white, and blue emerge as your lucky colors, complemented by moonstone or pearl and blue sapphire as auspicious gems. Saturdays and Mondays stand as fortuitous days, while numerical harmony resonates with 2, 11, 20, 29, 38, 47, 56, 65, and 74 — numbers symbolic of years marked by significant change.

Celestial Kin and Inspirations: Joining the celestial ranks of those born on January 20 are luminaries such as George Burns, Federico Fellini, Patricia Neal, David Lynch, Paula Patricio, Jamie Denton, Gary Barlow, and Jerry Swindall. Their diverse contributions echo the dynamic and innovative energies embedded in the essence of January 20 Capricorns.

Closing the Celestial Chapter: As the cosmic narrative unfolds, January 20 Capricorns emerge as pioneers of innovation, versatility, and sudden triumphs. The harmonious dance of Saturn, Uranus, and the Moon guides their journey, propelling them toward a destiny marked by uniqueness and the ability to navigate the unpredictable currents of life. May their path be illuminated by the sparks of Uranus as they weave the tapestry of their celestial destiny.

Astrological Profile for Those Born on January 21

Your Star Sign is Aquarius, Your personal ruling planets are Uranus and Jupiter.

Unlocking the Cosmic Tapestry: The Astrology of January 21 Aquarians

Title: "Elevated Paths and Artistic Instincts: Navigating the Cosmic Symphony of January 21 Aquarians"

Embark on a celestial exploration as we delve into the astrological nuances shaping the destiny of those born on January 21. Governed by the innovative energies of Uranus and the expansive influence of Jupiter, this Aquarian cohort emerges with a unique vibrational imprint linked to the number 21, opening gateways to elevated career trajectories and artistic pursuits.

Jupiter's Link to Number 21: The special vibration of January 21 Aquarians finds a connection to the planet Jupiter through the mystical number 21. This cosmic alignment promises an elevated and heightened career path, a celestial gift awaiting those who surmount initial hurdles. To maintain a buoyant mental attitude, the call to embrace instinctive artistic and poetic nature is sounded, offering a respite from an excess of work-centric tendencies associated with this birthdate.

Overcoming Opposition with Love: The astrological vibrations predict encounters with adversaries on the path of those born on January 21. However, a harmonious resonance suggests that opposition shall be conquered through the transformative power of love, paving the way for the attainment of responsible and influential positions. Love becomes the cosmic elixir that fuels triumph over challenges.

The Jan 21 Birthday Horizon: People born on January 21 emerge as happy and content individuals, navigating the spectrum of life's experiences. While early marriages may encounter turbulence, the financial industry becomes a fertile ground for success, culminating in mature capital in later years. Driven by an innate desire for achievement, there exists vulnerability to the erosion of dreams. Happiness, purpose, and a penchant for superficial entertainment characterize their journey.

Understanding Self-Needs and Overcoming Impulsiveness: Despite talent, modesty, and responsiveness, the quest to comprehend true needs remains a challenge for those born on January 21. A complex interplay of self-esteem, a commitment to the right path, and occasional sensitivity and impulsiveness marks their psychological landscape. Striking a balance becomes the cosmic imperative for these Aquarians.

Connectivity, Creativity, and Communication: A strong affinity with family and friends defines the social landscape of January 21-born individuals. Quick-witted, generous, and easy-going, they become magnets of popularity. Creativity, compassion, and adept communication skills amplify their influence. However, a subtle undercurrent of inflexibility serves as a cautionary note, urging them to navigate the waters of patience.

Lucky Colors, Gems, Days, and Numerical Signposts: Yellow, lemon, and sandy shades emerge as lucky colors, while yellow sapphire, citrine quartz, and golden topaz adorn the cosmic toolkit as auspicious gems. Thursdays, Tuesdays, and Sundays stand as fortuitous days, while numerical resonance aligns with 3, 12, 21, 30, 39, 48, 57, 66, and 75 — numbers etched in the celestial script denoting pivotal moments of change.

Celestial Kin and Inspirations: Sharing the cosmic birthdate with luminaries like George Orwell, Telly Savalas, Placido Domingo, Geena Davis, and Jennifer Keyte, January 21 Aquarians align with a tapestry of influential personalities. Their collective contributions echo the diverse and impactful energies embedded in the essence of January 21 Aquarians.

Closing the Celestial Chapter: As the celestial symphony unfolds, January 21 Aquarians emerge as architects of elevated paths, navigators of artistic instincts, and conquerors of opposition through the transformative power of love. The cosmic tapestry woven by Uranus and Jupiter sets the stage for a destiny marked by vibrancy, creativity, and responsible leadership. May their journey be guided by the harmonious interplay of celestial energies, as they navigate the cosmic currents of their unique existence.

Astrological Profile for Those Born on January 22

Your Star Sign is Aquarius, Your personal ruling planet is Uranus.
Navigating the Enigmatic Cosmos: Unraveling the Essence of January 22 Aquarians

Title: "Master Vibration and the Cusp of Mystery: Decoding the Cosmic Blueprint of January 22 Aquarians"

Embark on a celestial odyssey as we explore the astrological tapestry woven for those born on January 22, governed by the avant-garde energies of Uranus. Encapsulated within a master vibration, these individuals are destined for great attainment, their journey marked by originality of perspective, unwavering determination, and a capacity for uninterrupted hard work. However, the cosmic warnings echo caution against apathy and emphasize the need for practical application.

Master Vibration and Cosmic Attainment: Born under a master vibration, January 22 Aquarians possess the celestial key to unlocking great accomplishments in this life. Apathy emerges as their cosmic adversary, threatening to mar their originality, work capacity, and determination. The cosmic imperative resonates with the call to translate great potential into practical application, ensuring that the celestial gifts bestowed upon them find tangible expression.

Overcoming Apathy and Relationship Dynamics: While January 22-born individuals exhibit a tendency to over-worry, their perspectives in relationships are often misunderstood. A penchant for over-imagining the worst in any circumstance underscores their cosmic journey. The celestial counsel urges them to develop awareness and foresight, addressing challenges at their inception rather than succumbing to eleventh-hour revelations.

The Cusp of Mystery: Dubbed the Cusp of Mystery, January 22 marks a unique date on the cosmic calendar, influencing the characteristics shared by those born on this enigmatic day. Strengths and weaknesses intertwine, creating a nuanced portrait that aligns with the zodiac sign's influence and offers insights into romantic inclinations and independence.

Aquarian Dominion and Uranian Influences: The eleventh house, ruled by the sign of Aquarius, emerges as a space for friendship, higher goals, and dreams. Within this cosmic realm, social contact, friendly behavior, and openness flourish. Uranus, the ruling planet, assumes a role as the rebellious new star, guiding those born on January 22 towards mastery over their lower nature. Reliability, decisiveness, and the ability to express feelings with subtlety and intelligence become hallmarks of their cosmic identity.

Astrological Forecast for January 22: The Full Moon in the first half of the month unfurls a celestial tapestry promising positive developments for January 22-born individuals. Under the influence of Taurus, a helpful sign offering advice and support, the year becomes conducive to networking and self-promotion. While motivation for increased responsibility and independent work is amplified, the cosmic currents may present challenges in familial and relational spheres.

Lucky Colors, Gems, Days, and Numerical Signposts: Electric blue, electric white, and multi-colors emerge as lucky colors, weaving into the cosmic palette of January 22 Aquarians. Hessonite garnet and agate stand as auspicious gems, embodying the celestial energies that resonate with their essence. Sundays and Thursdays align as fortuitous days, while numerical resonance echoes through 4, 13, 22, 31, 40, 49, 58, 67, and 76 — numerical signposts marking moments of important change.

Celestial Kin and Inspirations: In the cosmic congregation of influential personalities born on January 22, luminaries like Francis Bacon, Gotthold Lessing, Lord Byron, D.W. Griffith, Piper Laurie, Stacey Dash, and others contribute to the celestial symphony, sharing common threads of cosmic influence with those born on this enigmatic date.

Closing the Celestial Chapter: As January 22 Aquarians navigate the cosmic currents, the master vibration and the Cusp of Mystery unveil a celestial blueprint destined for great attainment. The call to transcend apathy, navigate relationship dynamics with foresight, and embrace the cosmic gifts bestowed upon them resonates through the astrological echoes. May their journey be marked by the harmonious interplay of celestial energies, guiding them towards the cosmic heights inscribed in the cosmic script of their unique existence.

Astrological Profile for Those Born on January 23

Your Star Sign is Aquarius, Your personal ruling planets are Uranus and Mercury.

Harmony of Poetic Vibrations: Navigating the Cosmic Tapestry of January 23 Aquarians

Title: "A Symphony of Speech and Versatility: The Celestial Composition of January 23 Aquarians"

Embark on a celestial journey as we unravel the astrological intricacies woven into the essence of those born on January 23, governed by the harmonious energies of Uranus and Mercury. Poetic vibrations emanate from this date, harmonizing with spontaneous joy and happiness. Gifted in the art of speech, January 23-born individuals find their cosmic calling in teaching and communication, guided by a quick-learning spirit and an eternal zest for knowledge.

Poetic Vibrations and Gifted Speech: Born under the celestial influence of Uranus and Mercury, January 23 Aquarians exude poetic vibrations that resonate in their speech and expressions. Endowed with surprising linguistic gifts, they are urged to consider languages as a pastime or career. A quick learner and perpetual student of life, professions involving teaching or speech align seamlessly with their cosmic blueprint. Their persuasiveness and original problem-solving prowess mark them as celestial wordsmiths.

Versatility and Adaptability: The cosmic tapestry woven for January 23-born individuals promises a destiny brimming with life changes. However, their versatile and adaptable nature ensures that these shifts pose minimal challenges. A harmony of cosmic energies propels them through transformations, with the only caution being the impact of moods on their health. The celestial counsel encourages maintaining bright and breezy moods to safeguard their well-being.

Dependability and Eccentricity: While January 23-born individuals exhibit dependability, the influence of Aquarius injects a dose of eccentricity. High expectations may be harbored, and negative characteristics, such as irritability and grudge-holding tendencies, can surface. Recognizing these traits is crucial for maintaining healthy relationships. The delicate balance between dependability and eccentricity forms the canvas of their cosmic portrait.

Health and Lifestyle Considerations: Health assumes prime importance for those born on January 23, yet bad habits may pose challenges. Difficulty in adhering to advice for a healthier lifestyle may surface. Fussy food preferences call for a balanced diet, and regular check-ups become imperative. Their unique blend of masculine and feminine traits makes for an innovative and creative personality, but focus and clarity may require attention.

Social Influence and Luck: January 23 Aquarians wield a positive influence on others, attracting family, friends, and coworkers. Effort invested in relationships is vital for their endurance. Public recognition and new job opportunities may grace their path, with astrological insights guiding them toward creativity and innovation. The celestial currents underscore the impact of their astrological sign on luck and life's fortunes.

Lucky Colors, Gems, Days, and Numerical Signposts: The celestial palette of January 23 Aquarians is adorned with the lucky color green. Emerald, Aquamarine, or Jade emerge as auspicious gems, channeling cosmic energies. Wednesdays, Fridays, and Saturdays stand as fortuitous days, while the numerical resonance echoes through 5, 14, 23, 32, 41, 50, 59, 68, and 77 — numerical signposts guiding moments of important change.

Celestial Kin and Inspirations: Among the cosmic kin born on January 23, luminaries like Stendahl, Edouard Manet, Humphrey Bogart, Rutger Hauer, and others contribute to the celestial symphony. Their shared cosmic influences intertwine with the unique essence of January 23-born individuals, creating a celestial harmony.

Closing the Celestial Chapter: As January 23 Aquarians navigate the cosmic currents, their celestial composition echoes with the symphony of speech, versatility, and the poetic dance of Uranus and Mercury. Gifted communicators and perpetual learners, they traverse life's changes with adaptability, guided by the cosmic forces shaping their destiny. May their celestial journey be adorned with bright moods, harmonious relationships, and the creative flourish of their linguistic gifts inscribed in the cosmic script of their unique existence.

Astrological Profile for Those Born on January 24

Your Star Sign is Aquarius, Your personal ruling planets are Uranus and Venus.

Navigating the Cosmic Canvas: Insights into the Aquarian Essence of January 24 Birthdays

Title: "Harmony of Independence and Family Bonds: The Cosmic Canvas of January 24 Aquarians"

Embark on an astrological exploration as we unravel the celestial threads woven into the essence of those born on January 24, guided by the harmonious energies of Uranus and Venus. A compelling love for family intertwines with a dynamic pursuit of personal and professional endeavors, crafting a vibrant cosmic canvas for those celebrating this unique birth date.

Love of Family and Artistic Vibrations: For January 24-born Aquarians, a profound love of family is a guiding force. The cosmic energies of Uranus and Venus infuse their vibrations with social and artistic flair. Despite a mind prone to overstimulation from taking on too much, the motto "bite off more than you can chew and then chew like crazy" defines their approach to life. While an initial desire for an artistic career may be present, destiny does not necessarily tether them to this path.

Ideal Professions and Social Magnetism: Well-suited for public-facing roles, those born on January 24 thrive in areas such as public relations, advertising, and sales. Their successes often find support through influential women. The cosmic currents grant them a highly magnetic personality, abundant creativity, and a surplus of energy. The exciting vibrations they emanate contribute to their ability to make an impact in their chosen endeavors.

Health and Vibrancy: The overall health of January 24-born individuals is generally robust, although a potential weakness in the urinary tract may be constitutionally present. Vibrancy and energy characterize their physical well-being, aligning with the dynamic nature of their cosmic vibrations. The cosmic counsel encourages maintaining balance and addressing any constitutional vulnerabilities to ensure a healthy and fulfilling life journey.

Magnetic Personality and Creative Flow: A magnetic personality defines those born on January 24, accompanied by a healthy flow of creativity. They serve as examples to others and play a vital role in the growth and success of those around them. While charm is a hallmark trait, challenges arise in the form of potential self-centeredness, patronizing tendencies, and moments of frustration. Navigating these traits becomes essential for personal growth.

Astrological Insights for the Year: The January 24 Zodiac forecasts a year marked by intelligence, keen understanding of people, and an inclination toward recklessness with finances. Independence is a defining feature, urging caution in choosing relationships built on mutual respect and trust. Resolving inheritance issues and embracing karmic lessons from the past form crucial aspects of the cosmic guidance. Relationships may encounter rocky terrain, requiring compromises and emotional expression.

Lucky Colors, Gems, Days, and Numerical Signposts: The celestial palette for January 24 Aquarians is adorned with lucky colors such as white, cream, rose, and pink. Diamond, white sapphire, or quartz crystal emerge as auspicious gems. Fortuitous days include Wednesday, Friday, and Saturday, while the numerical resonance echoes through 6, 15, 24, 33, 42, 51, 60, 69, and 78 — signposts guiding moments of important change.

Celestial Kin and Inspirations: Among the cosmic kin born on January 24, luminaries like Edith Wharton, Ernest Borgnine, John Belushi, Tatyana Ali, and Mischa Barton contribute to the celestial symphony. Their shared cosmic influences intertwine with the unique essence of January 24-born individuals, creating a cosmic harmony.

Closing the Cosmic Chapter: As January 24 Aquarians navigate the celestial currents, their cosmic canvas pulsates with independence, family bonds, and a vibrant pursuit of success. Love for family and artistic vibrations infuse their journey, complemented by ideal professions and a magnetic personality. Challenges are embraced, and the cosmic guidance for the year encourages resilience, expression, and the resolution of karmic threads. May their cosmic journey be adorned with the harmonious strokes of family love, dynamic creativity, and the fulfillment of their unique cosmic destiny.

Astrological Profile for Those Born on January 25

Your Star Sign is Aquarius, Your personal ruling planets are Uranus and Neptune.

Unveiling the Aquarian Tapestry: A Dive into the Cosmic Currents of January 25 Birthdays

Title: "Aquarian Persuasion and Mystical Depths: Navigating the Cosmic Waves of January 25"

Embark on a celestial journey as we unravel the cosmic tapestry woven for those born on January 25, guided by the dynamic energies of Uranus and Neptune. With the power of persuasion and an innate connection to nature, these individuals find their path illuminated by teaching, advising, and the enchanting realm of water sports. Join us in exploring the mystical depths and cosmic influences that shape the unique essence of January 25-born Aquarians.

Persuasive Energies and Future Gains: Blessed with the gift of persuasion, those born on January 25 hold the power to captivate others through their convincing techniques. The cosmic energies on their birth day hint at future gains through roles in teaching, lecturing, and advisory positions. A magnetic aura surrounds them, drawing others to listen and learn from their insights.

Neptunian Vibes and Prophetic Dreams: The higher vibrations of Neptune infuse the lives of January 25-born individuals with vivid and prophetic dreams. This mystical influence may come as a surprise, opening a gateway to the ethereal realms. A deep love for nature, especially water, enhances their emotional vitality, and the possibility of engaging in water sports becomes a source of joy and rejuvenation.

Protection from Curses and Black Magic: The cosmic alignment on January 25 is said to offer protection from curses and black magic. This celestial shield adds an intriguing layer to the mystical nature of those born on this date, instilling a sense of safeguarding against unseen forces.

Birthday Horoscope Insights: The Birthday Horoscope for January 25 unveils two potential scenarios: one of happiness and another involving challenges in finding true love. A unique blend of signs, including Aries, Taurus, Cancer, Virgo, Libra, Scorpio, Pisces, Aquarius, and Leo, shapes the cosmic landscape. Despite occasional feelings of unfulfillment and a lack of confidence, exceptional money-making potential lies within, intertwined with the propensity for unexpected accidents and a penchant for reshuffling goals and priorities.

Aquarian Personality Traits: Typifying the Aquarian personality, those born on January 25 exude an appealing yet mysterious aura. Dreamy, introspective, and magnetic, they may grapple with introversion and challenges in interpersonal relationships. Navigating the cosmic currents, they often find solace in avoiding conflicting energies and embracing a more solitary existence.

Lucky Charms and Cosmic Guidance: The cosmic palette for January 25-born individuals is adorned with darker green shades, reflecting their connection to nature and the enigmatic depths of Neptune. Turquoise, cats eye chrysoberyl, and tigers eye emerge as auspicious gems, amplifying their cosmic energies. Mondays and Thursdays stand as lucky days, while the numerical resonance echoes through 7, 16, 25, 34, 43, 52, 61, 70, and 79 — guiding lights in moments of important change.

Celestial Kin and Inspirations: Among the celestial kin born on January 25, luminaries such as Robert Burns, W. Somerset Maugham,

Virginia Woolf, and Christine Lakin contribute to the cosmic symphony. Their shared cosmic influences intertwine with the unique essence of January 25-born individuals, creating a harmonious cosmic connection.

Closing the Cosmic Chapter: As January 25-born Aquarians traverse the cosmic waves, their tapestry is painted with the strokes of persuasive energies, mystical depths, and protective cosmic influences. The dynamic blend of Uranus and Neptune shapes their journey, inspiring roles in teaching and advisory realms. Challenges and blessings interweave, offering opportunities for growth, unexpected financial gains, and a unique connection to the ethereal. May their cosmic voyage be illuminated by the allure of water, the power of persuasion, and the celestial protection that guards their path.

Astrological Profile for Those Born on January 26

Your Star Sign is Aquarius, Your personal ruling planets are Uranus and Saturn.

Unlocking the Cosmic Code: Navigating the Fortunes of January 26 Birthdays

Title: "Aquarian Resilience and Creative Forces: Decoding the Cosmic Tapestry of January 26"

Embark on a cosmic exploration as we decode the celestial messages woven into the destiny of those born on January 26, guided by the dynamic influences of Uranus and Saturn. Steeped in the karmic essence of strength through tribulation, these individuals face a journey marked by dedication, loyalty, and tenacity. Join us in unraveling the cosmic tapestry that shapes the unique essence of January 26-born Aquarians.

Karmic Strength Through Tribulation: For those born on January 26, the cosmic alignment denotes a journey of karmic strength through tribulation. While the birth date may not be deemed traditionally lucky, it signals that even small successes may require diligent effort. A sense of difficulty in receiving support from others, coupled with the perception of reluctance from relatives, becomes a cornerstone of their journey.

Dedication, Loyalty, and Tenacity: The better traits of their nature include unwavering dedication, loyalty, and a tenacious spirit to see endeavors through to completion. However, the cosmic landscape also presents challenges in the form of inner demons, battling depression, and fostering a somewhat pessimistic outlook on life.

Creative Talents and Dramatic Flair: Infused with a natural dramatic flair and creative talents, those born on January 26 gradually develop a spiritual attitude later in life. The cosmic currents encourage leveraging these innate gifts to navigate challenges and embark on a transformative journey toward enlightenment.

Love Lesson: "Do Not Demand and Ye Shall Receive": In matters of love, the cosmic lesson for January 26-born individuals is succinctly put as "do not demand and ye shall receive." Balancing expectations and cultivating a more selfless approach becomes a pivotal aspect of their cosmic journey in the realm of relationships.

Alignment with Gemini, Pisces, and Capricorn: While sharing similarities with the opposites of Gemini, Pisces, and Capricorn, January 26 stands as a day of great energy and strength. The individuals born on this date exhibit high levels of creativity and passion, tempered with a touch of stubbornness and independence. The journey is marked by a commitment to relationships and an unwavering effort towards success.

Ambition and Leadership: Those born on January 26 are driven by ambition, with far-reaching goals that propel them toward success. Their unquestionable talent for business, coupled with creativity, positions them as effective leaders. However, caution is advised against hasty decisions and impulsive actions that may stem from emotional fluctuations.

Lucky Charms and Cosmic Signposts: The cosmic palette for January 26-born individuals is adorned with deep blue and black hues, reflecting their reservoir of strength and resilience. Blue sapphire, lapis lazuli, and amethyst emerge as lucky gems, infusing their journey with protective energies. Wednesdays, Fridays, and Saturdays stand as lucky days, while the numerical resonance echoes through 8, 17, 26, 35, 44, 53, 62, and 71 — guiding lights in moments of important change.

Celestial Kin and Cosmic Connections: Among the celestial kin born on January 26, luminaries such as Douglas MacArthur, Hans Holzer, Paul Newman, Eartha Kitt, Jules Feiffer, Scott Glen, Ellen DeGeneres, and Vince Carter contribute to the cosmic symphony. Their shared cosmic influences intertwine with the unique essence of January 26-born individuals, creating a harmonious cosmic connection.

Closing the Cosmic Chapter: As January 26-born Aquarians tread the cosmic path, their tapestry is interwoven with themes of karmic strength, dedication, and creative resilience. The dynamic interplay of Uranus and Saturn shapes their journey, fostering a commitment to relationships, ambitious pursuits, and a transformative evolution toward spiritual enlightenment. May their cosmic voyage be guided by the cosmic forces of deep blue, black, and the numerological signposts that illuminate the path of January 26.

Astrological Profile for Those Born on January 27

Your Star Sign is Aquarius, Your personal ruling planets are Uranus and Mars.

Embracing Uniqueness: Navigating the Cosmic Currents of January 27 Birthdays

Title: "Aquarian Visionaries: Unveiling the Unique Spirit of January 27"

Embark on a celestial journey as we unveil the cosmic secrets woven into the essence of those born on January 27, guided by the celestial dance of Uranus and Mars. Labeled as the "unique spirit," these individuals bear a psychic and clairvoyant streak, offering insights into their practical prowess and potential ascent to positions of power. Join us in decoding the cosmic currents that define the unique spirit of January 27-born Aquarians.

The Unique Spirit Unveiled: Individuals born on January 27 carry the moniker of the "unique spirit." Their date of birth aligns with a psychic and clairvoyant streak, hinting at an innate ability to tap into the unseen realms. However, the practical side of their nature opens doors to public office and positions of influence, emphasizing a duality that combines intuitive insight with worldly pragmatism.

Creative Minds for Social Welfare: Driven by a creative mind and a genuine desire to assist others, those born on January 27 find purpose in contributing to social welfare and engaging in the helping and healing professions. Their presence in these realms becomes a source of inspiration and positive impact, showcasing a unique blend of altruism and inventive thinking.

Energy Sensitivity and Psychic Protection: While blessed with a unique spirit, individuals born on this date may experience fluctuations in energy levels. Their aura mirrors the positive or negative vibrations in their environment. To navigate these nuances, learning to protect oneself psychically becomes a valuable skill, ensuring that their unique gifts remain a source of strength rather than vulnerability.

Birthday Horoscope Insights: A January 27 birthday horoscope unveils a personality marked by uniqueness, cleverness, and thoughtfulness. Often underestimated, these individuals possess a strong will and the capacity for significant achievements with focused determination. Maturity and patience are emphasized, urging them to allow time for outcomes and to embrace compromise when necessary.

Gifted Connections and Ethical Integrity: Individuals born on January 27 are gifted with the ability to connect with diverse personalities. Politeness, an appreciation for physical appeal, and a strong sense of integrity set the foundation for meaningful relationships. Their sense of ethics becomes a guiding force, inspiring others through the manifestation of valued qualities.

Lucky Charms and Celestial Signposts: The cosmic palette for January 27-born individuals is adorned with red, maroon, scarlet, and autumn tones — hues that reflect their vibrant and dynamic spirits. Red coral and garnet emerge as lucky gems, infusing protective energies into their cosmic journey. Mondays, Tuesdays, and Thursdays stand as lucky days, while the numerical resonance echoes through 9, 18, 27, 36, 45, 54, 63, and 72 — guiding lights in moments of important change.

Celestial Kin and Cosmic Connections: Among the celestial kin born on January 27, luminaries such as Mozart, Lewis Carroll, William II, Donna Reed, Troy Donahue, Mimi Rogers, Bridget Fonda, Tracy Lawrence, Fann Wong, and Marat Safin contribute to the cosmic symphony. Their shared cosmic influences intertwine with the unique essence of January 27-born individuals, creating a harmonious cosmic connection.

Closing the Celestial Chapter: As January 27-born Aquarians navigate the cosmic currents, their unique spirit stands as a beacon of inspiration. The interplay of psychic insights, practical prowess, and a commitment to social welfare defines their cosmic journey. May the vibrant hues of red and maroon, coupled with the protective energies of red coral and garnet, guide them through the celestial dance. Embrace the uniqueness, celebrate the journey, and let the cosmic currents carry you toward realms yet unseen.

Astrological Profile for Those Born on January 28

Your Star Sign is Aquarius, Your personal ruling planets are Uranus and Sun.

Navigating Contradictions: The Cosmic Tapestry of January 28 Birthdays

Title: "Aquarian Pioneers: Embracing the Contradictions of January 28"

Embark on a cosmic exploration as we delve into the intriguing tapestry of those born on January 28, guided by the harmonious dance of Uranus and the Sun. In this astrological profile, we unravel the unique vibration of the number 28, the interplay of contradictory forces, and the transformative journey toward self-confidence and independence.

Contradictions and Unusual Vibrations: Individuals born on January 28 emanate an unusual vibration, where the number 28 symbolizes contradiction. The harmonic interplay of the Moon and Saturn introduces challenges to the expression of creativity and emotional urges. A key lesson is to resist suppressing inner excitement and inspiration. Embracing independence and asserting one's voice become essential components of this cosmic journey.

Conquering Inner Fears and Embracing Confidence: Any feelings of depression or dullness may trace back to earlier issues with the mother. The cosmic mandate for those born on January 28 is to conquer inner fears and cultivate the confidence to stride boldly into a radiant future. This transformative journey involves shedding inhibitions and embracing the full spectrum of emotions.

Determined, Persistent, and Adventurous: The January 28 birthday horoscope paints a portrait of individuals characterized by determination, persistence, and a thirst for adventure. Organized and well-groomed, they exhibit a balance between order and spontaneity. However, the energy may not always manifest positively, with tendencies toward quick temper and impulsiveness. Evaluating career paths and remaining open to change becomes a focal point for personal growth.

Wandering Minds and the Journey to Wisdom: As Sun sign Aquarians, those born on January 28 navigate the challenges of wandering minds and a tendency to focus on the past. Attention easily drifts, and cultivating a sense of common sense becomes crucial. Despite occasional feelings of detachment, the journey toward happiness and fulfillment lies in turning weaknesses into strengths and making wiser life choices.

Pragmatic Approach and Overcoming Obstacles: January 28 individuals approach life with pragmatism, preferring practicality over heedless pursuits. They find joy in leading and overcoming obstacles. Classes and learning opportunities align with their interests, requiring a touch of courage. Mondays hold a special resonance, offering a sense of happiness and fulfillment.

Lucky Charms and Celestial Signposts: The cosmic palette for January 28-born individuals features copper and gold — hues reflecting both warmth and resilience. Ruby emerges as a lucky gem, infusing strength and vitality into their cosmic journey. Fortunate days include Sunday, Monday, and Thursday, with numerical resonance echoing through 1, 10, 19, 28, 37, 46, 55, 64, 73, and 82 — signposts of important change.

Celestial Kin and Cosmic Connections: Among the celestial kin born on January 28, luminaries such as Artur Rubinstein, Jackson

Pollock, Sarah McLachlan, Joey Fatone, Nick Carter, and Elijah Wood contribute to the cosmic symphony. Their shared cosmic influences intertwine with the unique essence of January 28-born individuals, creating a harmonious cosmic connection.

Closing the Celestial Chapter: As those born on January 28 navigate the contradictions of their cosmic journey, they emerge as Aquarian pioneers, embracing challenges, fostering independence, and transforming inner fears into confidence. May the hues of copper and gold guide them through moments of contradiction, and may the energy of ruby infuse their path with strength. Embrace the contradictions, navigate the cosmic currents, and let the celestial dance lead you toward the brilliance of self-discovery.

Astrological Profile for Those Born on January 29

Your Star Sign is Aquarius, Your personal ruling planets are Uranus and Moon.

Riding the Lightning: Navigating the Cosmic Currents of January 29 Birthdays

Title: "Aquarian Sparks: Embracing Lightning-Quick Ambitions on January 29"

Embark on a celestial journey as we unravel the astrological tapestry of those born on January 29, guided by the electrifying dance of Uranus and the Moon. In this cosmic profile, we explore the unique energies that fuel lightning-quick reactions, the quest for self-confidence, and the dynamic interplay of ambitions that define this distinctive group.

Lightning-Quick Reactions and Ambitious Sparks: Individuals born on January 29 ride the cosmic lightning, with reactions that defy the conventional pace of life. Ambitions burn brightly, and the motto "more is better" encapsulates their dynamic approach. The cosmic guidance encourages a balance between the thrill of sensation and the wisdom of tempering desires, urging a crawl before a walk in the pursuit of goals.

Family Dynamics and Observant Friendships: Family life for those born on January 29 may witness sudden outbursts of emotion and anger. The cosmic energy prompts a need for loved ones to accommodate these fiery moments. In friendships, caution is advised, as not all associates may prove reliable. Powers of observation become valuable tools in scrutinizing true intentions and conserving energy for meaningful connections.

Focus on Self-Confidence: The crux of the January 29 birthday horoscope lies in the pursuit of self-confidence. The quest for self-esteem is insatiable, and independence emerges as the ultimate goal. Relationships may be a complex landscape, with a preference for companionship over solitude. Strengths include impartiality, adaptability, and a fun-loving nature, while weaknesses manifest as hesitancy, indecision, and an inclination to be overly compliant.

Adaptable Explorers with a Risk-Taking Spirit: Born on January 29, Aquarians exhibit a distinctive personality marked by adaptability and a love for exploration. Thriving in unconventional environments, they cherish diversity in friendships. Their active, lovable, and risk-taking spirit propels them forward, yet a concern for material security may linger. While financial situations are generally secure, indecision may cloud important decisions.

Overcoming Challenges with Compassion: Overcoming challenges involves overcoming an overly active side and addressing concerns about material security. The January 29-born individual may grapple with indecision, losing track of time, or engaging in pursuits lacking personal interest. Patience becomes a virtue in navigating these challenges. By fostering compassion and understanding, they can transform weaknesses into strengths.

Celestial Hues and Lucky Charms: The cosmic palette for January 29-born individuals features the soothing colors of cream, white, and green. Moonstone or pearl emerge as lucky gems, reflecting the ethereal connection to the Moon. Fortunate days include Monday, Thursday, and Sunday, with numerical resonance echoing through 2, 11, 20, 29, 38, 47, 56, 65, and 74 — celestial signposts of important change.

Celestial Kin and Cosmic Connections: Among the celestial kin born on January 29, luminaries such as Swedenborg, William

McKinley, Oprah Winfrey, Tom Selleck, and Matthew Ashford contribute to the cosmic symphony. Their shared cosmic influences intertwine with the unique essence of January 29-born individuals, creating a harmonious cosmic connection.

Closing the Celestial Chapter: As those born on January 29 navigate the lightning-quick currents of their cosmic journey, they emerge as Aquarian sparks, embracing ambitions with a dynamic energy. May the celestial hues of cream, white, and green guide them through the storms of indecision, and may the lucky gems of moonstone and pearl illuminate their path. Ride the lightning, seek self-confidence, and let the cosmic dance lead you toward the brilliance of self-discovery.

Astrological Profile for Those Born on January 30

Your Star Sign is Aquarius, Your personal ruling planets are Uranus and Jupiter.

Radiant Hearts and Expansive Spirits: Navigating the Cosmos of January 30 Birthdays

Title: "Sunshine Souls: Illuminating the Zodiac with January 30 Radiance"

Embark on a cosmic exploration of the vibrant energies surrounding those born on January 30, guided by the celestial dance of Uranus and Jupiter. This astrological profile unveils the pure and generous hearts that radiate sunshine, offering sound judgment and magnanimity. As we delve into the cosmic tapestry, we encounter warnings against uncalculated risks and glimpses of enhanced future luck, urging individuals to remain content with their inner selves.

Pure Hearts and Sound Judgments: Individuals born on January 30 embody pure and generous hearts, emanating sunshine to brighten the world. With a magnanimous spirit and sound judgment, they navigate life's intricacies. The vibrations surrounding these souls hint at a destiny brimming with enhanced luck for the future, and their zeal promises to benefit society at some stage.

Trusting Intuitions and Expansive Natures: The cosmic guidance encourages a deep trust in inner intuitions, recognizing them as reliable compasses. While challenges may not easily bring them down, there's a caution against the expansive nature tempting individuals to take uncalculated risks. The cosmic message advises steering clear of gambling tendencies, offering a reminder that destiny may swing between winning big and losing big. Contentment with the inner self becomes a guiding principle.

Compatibility Insights and Aristocratic Bearings: Born on January 30, these individuals may find challenges in making a life for themselves. Privacy and intimacy are craved, and compatibility in romantic relationships is heightened with those born on the 18th and 24th. Despite an aristocratic bearing, they maintain a friendly and accessible demeanor. Uranus, inspiring optimism, takes the lead in their cosmic journey, pushing against encroaching pessimism. Love, marked by demands and occasional jealousy, flourishes through shared time.

Optimism, Forgiveness, and Idealism: Optimism, principled ideals, and a forgiving nature define those born on January 30. Open to accepting others as they are, they extend this understanding to diverse perspectives. While quick to forgive, they may grapple with the challenge of accepting imperfections in others. The horoscope gains depth when aligned with personal goals and aspirations, shaping a holistic understanding of their cosmic path.

Lucky Hues, Gems, and Celestial Signposts: Yellow, lemon, and sandy shades paint the lucky colors of January 30-born individuals, infusing positivity into their cosmic aura. Yellow sapphire, citrine quartz, and golden topaz emerge as auspicious gems. The cosmic rhythm resonates strongly on Thursday, Tuesday, and Sunday. Numeric echoes guide the journey, marked by the significance of 3, 12, 21, 30, 39, 48, 57, 66, and 75 — celestial signposts of change and growth.

Celestial Kin and Illuminated Souls: Among the celestial kin sharing the radiance of January 30, luminaries like F.D. Roosevelt, Gene Hackman, Vanessa Redgrave, and Christian Bale contribute to the cosmic mosaic. Their shared journey, guided by Uranus and Jupiter, intertwines with the unique essence of those born on January 30, forming an illuminated tapestry of shared cosmic energies.

Closing the Celestial Chapter: As January 30-born individuals navigate the cosmic currents, they emerge as sunshine souls, casting their radiance with pure hearts and sound judgment. May the celestial hues of yellow and lemon guide them through expansive choices, and may the auspicious gems of citrine quartz and golden topaz illuminate their cosmic path. Trusting intuitions, avoiding uncalculated risks, and finding contentment within become the cosmic mantras. Ride the waves of enhanced luck, embrace compatibility in love, and let the inner radiance shine brightly in the cosmic dance of self-discovery.

Astrological Profile for Those Born on January 31

Your Star Sign is Aquarius, Your personal ruling planet is Uranus.
Revolutionary Spirits and Magnetic Auras: Navigating the Cosmos of January 31 Birthdays

Title: "Beyond Tradition: Embracing the Aquarian Radiance of January 31"

Embark on a cosmic journey delving into the revolutionary spirits and magnetic auras of those born on January 31, guided by the celestial dance with Uranus. This astrological profile unveils a unique essence that challenges societal norms and embraces a positive view of life. From a desire for independence to an attraction to like-minded individuals, January 31 souls radiate a progressive mindset, physical mobility, and a love for rugged outdoor activities.

Revolutionary Essence and Unconventional Paths: Born on January 31, individuals are blessed with a revolutionary spirit, rejecting the conventional norms of society. The cosmic influence of Uranus fuels a desire for independence, occasionally leading to feelings of isolation. Despite overwhelming emotions, a generally positive view of life prevails, marked by big plans and experiences of sudden reversals coupled with successes.

Aim for the Horizon: The cosmic compass of those born on January 31 points towards the horizon. With a preference for the big picture, they navigate life with a progressive mind and physical mobility. Rugged sports and outdoor activities become avenues for the search for inner meaning, channeling the overwhelming feelings within.

Unwavering Love and Attraction to Like Minds: In matters of the heart, individuals born on this day give their all. Attracted to those of the same sign, they share a common spirit of challenging societal rules. This mutual rebelliousness creates magnetic connections, making them appealing and admirable to others. While a strong need for acceptance exists, their uniqueness stands as a testament to their revolutionary essence.

Charming, Creative, and Intuitive Minds: People born on January 31 are often surrounded by nature, drawing inspiration from its beauty. Intelligent, creative, and intuitive, they communicate effectively and make decisions based on intuition. The magnetic spirit within them fosters teamwork and attraction, contributing to their ability to lead and inspire.

Lucky Hues, Gems, and Celestial Signposts: Electric blue, electric white, and multi-colors paint the lucky hues for those born on January 31, enhancing their cosmic aura. Hessonite garnet and agate emerge as auspicious gems, grounding their energies. The cosmic rhythm beats strongest on Sunday and Thursday, guiding their celestial journey. Numeric echoes of 4, 13, 22, 31, 40, 49, 58, 67, and 76 serve as celestial signposts, marking years of change and growth.

Celestial Kin and Inspirational Figures: Among the celestial kin sharing the radiant energies of January 31, luminaries like Franz Schubert, Carol Channing, and Justin Timberlake contribute to the cosmic tapestry. Their shared journey, intertwined with the unique essence of those born on January 31, forms an inspirational mosaic of shared cosmic energies.

Closing the Celestial Chapter: As January 31-born individuals navigate the cosmic currents, they embody revolutionary spirits challenging societal norms. May their positive view of life fuel big plans and triumphs amid sudden reversals. Aiming for the horizon, they explore rugged terrains of inner meaning and channel overwhelming emotions through physical mobility. Love becomes an unwavering force, attracting like minds and forming magnetic connections in the cosmic dance of self-discovery.

Zodiac : Tropical					Placidus Orb : 0			
☉	Sun	♈	Aries	11°29'		I ASC	♉ Taurus	15°06'
☽	Moon	♑	Capricorn	7°37'		II	♊ Gemini	13°12'
☿	Mercury	♓	Pisces	18°09'		III	♋ Cancer	4°07'
♀	Venus	♈	Aries	28°59'		IV	♋ Cancer	24°28'
♂	Mars	♑	Capricorn	2°12'		V	♌ Leo	18°58'
♃	Jupiter	♓	Pisces	9°20'		VI	♍ Virgo	24°32'
♄	Saturn	♐	Sagittarius	9°34' R		VII	♏ Scorpio	15°06'
♅	Uranus	♐	Sagittarius	22°22' R		VIII	♐ Sagittarius	13°12'
♆	Neptune	♑	Capricorn	5°49'		IX	♑ Capricorn	4°07'
♇	Pluto	♏	Scorpio	6°39' R		X MC	♑ Capricorn	24°28'
⚸	Lilith	♊	Gemini	3°47'		XI	♒ Aquarius	18°58'
☊	N Node	♈	Aries	29°59'		XII	♓ Pisces	24°32'

Conclusion:

Embracing the Cosmic Symphony of January Souls

In the celestial dance of stars and the symphony of numbers, we've embarked on a journey through the intricate tapestry of January souls. From the fiery pioneers of Aries to the grounded architects of Capricorn, and the harmonious blend of both, each January soul is a unique cosmic masterpiece. As we conclude this cosmic exploration, let's reflect on the essence of our shared voyage.

The Cosmic Kaleidoscope: January souls, envision yourselves as cosmic kaleidoscopes, shaped by the dance of planets and elements. The fiery spirit of Aries ignites your passion, while the grounded wisdom of Capricorn steadies your hand. The elements paint your soul with vibrant hues, creating a kaleidoscope of personalities that grace the world with unique strengths and quirks.

Unlocking Potentials and Navigating Challenges: We've unraveled the hidden potential within you, from pioneering spirits with strategic minds to resilient trailblazers with a deep well of loyalty. Yet, the cosmic journey is not without challenges. We've equipped you with the inner compass to navigate the storms, turn obstacles into opportunities, and emerge stronger with each twist and turn.

A Symphony of Numbers and Tarot Whispers: Through the language of numbers, we've decoded the cosmic puzzle of your birthdate, revealing the guiding star of your life path and the vibrant voices of your soul urge and destiny numbers. In the hushed corners of the cosmic library, we've explored the mystical whispers of the tarot, allowing its symbolism to illuminate the hidden pathways of your January personality.

The Call to Shine: As we stand at the end of this cosmic journey, remember that challenges are not roadblocks; they are guideposts on your path to self-discovery. Embrace your unique brilliance, explore your hidden talents, and let the world witness the radiant light of your cosmic dance. Shine, January soul, and illuminate the world with the magic woven into your very being.

The Ever-Unfolding Story: This book is not the end but a beginning—an invitation to continue the exploration of your cosmic self. Your story is ever-unfolding, a tale written in the language of stars and numbers, painted with the hues of your unique personality. May the cosmic symphony continue to play, and may you dance to the rhythm of your own celestial melody.

As the pages of this cosmic guide gently close, carry forward the wisdom, embrace the challenges, and let your January light shine brightly, casting a luminous glow on the canvas of the universe. Until we meet again in the cosmic dance of life, January souls, may your journey be filled with discovery, growth, and the boundless magic of the cosmic symphony.

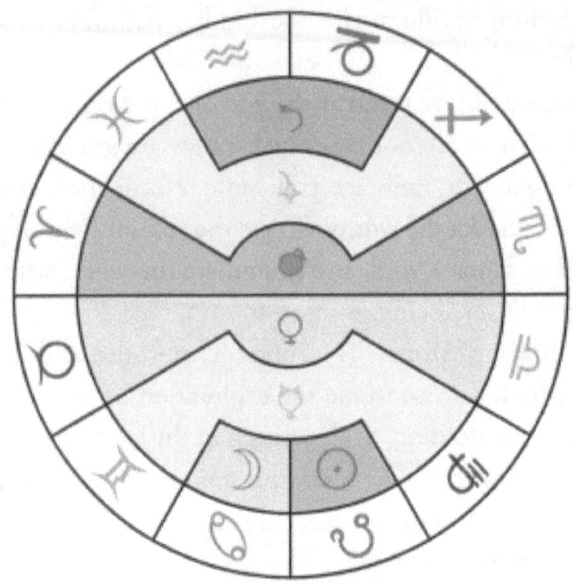

Contact the astrologer
Dear Reader

We extend our sincere thanks to you, dear readers, for embarking on this astrological journey with us. Your curiosity, engagement, and trust have made this exploration of the Zodiac sign Cancer all the more fulfilling.

In these pages, we have delved into the essence of the Cancer sign, unveiling its secrets, traits, and the horoscope for 2024. We've ventured through the depths of emotion, explored the intricacies of relationships, and discovered the likes and dislikes of a Cancer individual. All of this would not have been possible without your interest and presence.

Your quest for knowledge and self-discovery is what fuels our passion for astrology, and we are grateful to have been your guides in this cosmic voyage. We hope that the insights and wisdom shared in these pages serve as a guiding light in your life.

We invite you to explore our other books, each dedicated to a unique Zodiac sign and various aspects of astrology. Whether you seek to deepen your understanding of the stars or uncover the mysteries of other signs, you'll find a wealth of knowledge waiting for you.

Should you have any questions, insights, or simply wish to connect with us, please don't hesitate to reach out.

You can contact us via **WhatsApp at +1 829-205-5456** or **email us at danielsanjurjo47@gmail.com.**

May the stars continue to shine brightly on your path, and may your journey through the Zodiac signs be filled with enlightenment, growth, and harmony. **Sincerely Daniel Sanjurjo**

Did you love Cancer Zodiac Sign 2024? Then you should read The Dreams Interpretation Book[1] by Daniel Sanjurjo!

About the Author

Daniel Sanjurjo is a passionate author who delves into the realms of astrology and self-help. With a gift for exploring the celestial and the human psyche, Daniel's books are celestial journeys of self-discovery and personal growth. Join the cosmic odyssey with this insightful writer.

Don't miss out!

Visit the website below and you can sign up to receive emails whenever Daniel Sanjurjo publishes a new book. There's no charge and no obligation.

https://books2read.com/r/B-A-WQHBB-ENNSC

BOOKS 2 READ

Connecting independent readers to independent writers.

Did you love *The Secret Language of Birthdays Profiles - January Personality Insights.*? Then you should read *Capricorn 2024*[1] by Daniel Sanjurjo!

Hello, Capricorn enthusiasts, brace yourselves for a journey into the heart of 2024! This book is your go-to guide for unraveling the celestial mysteries that lie ahead, and we've broken it all down in a language that's as clear as a sunny day.

First things first, we'll dig into the roots of your zodiac sign, uncovering its intriguing history and mythical tales. Ever wondered why Capricorn is associated with the sea-goat or how time got tangled into the cosmic equation? We've got the scoop, and it's as fascinating as it gets!

1. https://books2read.com/u/496M60

2. https://books2read.com/u/496M60

Next on the agenda – your unique personality traits. From your rock-solid determination to managing that ambitious spirit, we're covering the whole spectrum. Plus, we'll spill the cosmic beans on how you connect with other zodiac signs – the good, the challenging, and the downright interesting.

And that's not all – we'll dive into the hues and gemstones that sync with your Capricorn vibes. Curious about career paths that align with your hardworking nature? We've got the lowdown, whether you're eyeing a leadership role or delving into finance.

But hold tight, we're not stopping there. Ready to navigate the twists and turns of your love life? We've got your back, and for the spicy details, we're delving into Capricorn's romantic prowess – it's about to get intriguing!

Now, the pièce de résistance – your 2024 horoscope. Wondering what the stars have in store for your finances, relationships, and well-being? We've got the details, and we're delivering it in plain and simple English. And for all the Capricorn students out there, get ready to shine because the stars are aligning in your favor!

So, buckle up, Capricorn aficionados! This book is your cosmic roadmap for 2024. It's like having a chat with the universe – straightforward, enjoyable, and brimming with celestial wisdom. Let's make this year one to remember!

Also by Daniel Sanjurjo

Birthdays Profiles
The Secret Language of Birthdays Profiles - January Personality
Insights.

Zodiaco
Aries 2024 Mes Por Mes
Tauro 2024 Mes Por Mes
Géminis 2024 Mes Por Mes
Cáncer 2024 Mes Por Mes
Leo 2024 Mes Por Mes:
Virgo 2024 Mes Por Mes
Libra 2024 Mes Por Mes
Escorpio 2024 Mes Por Mes
Sagitario 2024 Mes Por Mes
Capricornio 2024 Mes Por Mes
Acuario 2024 Mes Por Mes
Piscis 2024: Un Viaje Celestial
Piscis 2024 Mes Por Mes

Zodiac world

Aries Revealed 2024
Taurus 2024
Leo 2024
Gemini 2024
Cancer horoscope 2024
Virgo 2024
Scorpio 2024
Sagittarius 2024
Capricorn 2024
Aquarius 2024

Standalone
Cosmic Revelations 2024
Dreams Interpretation Guide
Explorando Mis Sueños: Descubre el Mundo Fascinante de tu Mente
Nocturna